Mind Your Tongue

Books by William E. Hulme
published by The Westminster Press

Mind Your Tongue:
Communication in the Family

Vintage Years:
Growing Older with Meaning and Hope

Mid-Life Crises (Christian Care Books)

Mind
Your Tongue
Communication in the Family

William E. Hulme

The Westminster Press
Philadelphia

© 1988 William E. Hulme

Book design by Gene Harris

First edition

Published by The Westminster Press®
Philadelphia, Pennsylvania

PRINTED IN THE UNITED STATES OF AMERICA

9 8 7 6 5 4 3 2 1

Library of Congress Cataloging-in-Publication Data

Hulme, William Edward, 1920-
    Mind your tongue : communication in the family / William E. Hulme.
— 1st ed.
    p.   cm.
    ISBN 0-664-24087-9 (pbk).
    1. Communication in the family—United States. 2. Family—United States—Religious life. 3. Interpersonal relations. I. Title.
HQ536.H85   1988
646.7'8—dc19   87-30042
                                                  CIP

Contents

1

The Puzzle
of the Tongue

"Shut up!" Jack Packer directed this familiar order, with all its usual heat, to his ten-year-old son, who had been nattering to his father about a TV program he had been forbidden to see. Eight or nine years ago, Jack was grasping for any indication that little Tommy was learning to talk. When Tommy's talking ability finally developed, the Packers were much relieved. Now Jack tells this same child to be quiet.

Our grandson is learning to talk. Obviously he has the potential for speech. But that potential will not be realized if he doesn't hear other human beings speaking. In our grandchild's case he hears two different kinds of speaking, because his father speaks Spanish to him and his nursery school teacher speaks English, as does his mother, and he listens as his mother and his father speak Spanish together. I believe he will know intuitively to use Spanish with his father and English with his teacher, and perhaps also with his mother. We shall wait and see.

The Role of Language in Culture

English and Spanish are not just words. They represent the culture, history, and pride of specific peoples. In fact, language is often the symbol of a people's identity. In Texas, for example, with its large Latin population, the question of using Spanish as well as English in the public schools arouses strong emotions, both among those for whom Spanish is a first language as well as among those whose mother tongue is English.

Canada has accommodated its French- and English-speaking populations by officially using both languages. The strong passions that perpetuate the Welsh language in Wales and the Gaelic language in Ireland indicate the place that language plays in preserving a people's identity.

With this identity comes self-esteem, pride as a people, and hope. My mother was a first-generation American. Her German immigrant father would not converse with any of his children unless they used German—even though he could speak English. And though he was completely deaf in his later years he would go only to the German-language communion service at church.

People are also identified by their language with a specific social class. This class identity of speech is the theme of George Bernard Shaw's play *Pygmalion*, which later became the basis for the popular musical *My Fair Lady*. Eliza Doolittle is transformed from a working-class flower seller to a cultured Englishwoman through Professor Higgins's success in changing her language patterns and pronunciations.

In the New Testament the apostle Peter on the night of Christ's arrest is in great danger of being exposed outside the high priest's courtyard as a follower of Christ because, as a Galilean in Judea, his "accent betrays" him (Matt. 26:73).

In the Old Testament the difficulty of pronouncing words like a native became the means for winning a battle. To fight against the Gileadites, the Ephraimites attempted to cross the river Jordan into Gileadite territory by posing as Gileadites. As peoples within the same Hebrew nation they could not be distinguished from each other by physical appearance. However, the Gileadites knew that the Ephraimites could not pronounce the Gileadite *sh*. So each time an Ephraimite was apprehended passing over the Jordan pretending to be a Gileadite and was asked by the Gileadite guard to say *Shibboleth*, the poor chap could only say *Sibboleth*, so he was executed on the spot (Judg. 12:1–6).

People from language traditions other than English find it difficult to pronounce the English *th*. We all have the same speech organs—tongue, lips, mouth, and vocal cords. But how we use them depends on our development in a particular language tradition. Once we have developed these speech patterns it is extremely difficult to alter them when learning another language without our accent betraying us.

Speech, with all of its significance for cultural and ethnic identity, is a distinctly human ability distinguishing us from other forms of life. While we are learning more and more about the communication patterns of chimpanzees and dolphins, and are often amazed by the ability of our animal pets to understand us, our human ability to speak is obviously a great advance over these other creatures.

A Mixed Blessing

Yet speaking is considered a mixed blessing. In fact, most of our "figures of speech" about speech are negative. Like the familiar "shut up," many put-downs on speech are family oriented: button your lip, keep your mouth shut, stifle yourself! I remember as a child being told "Halt's maul!" (Stop your mouth). All these expressions imply that closing down our organs of speech will be a blessing.

Words are obviously an ambiguous asset. They can be used as weapons to hurt and hurt deeply. In his Sermon on the Mount, Jesus used the label "fool" as the epitome of wounding words. "Whoever says, 'You fool!' shall be liable to the hell of fire" (Matt. 5:22).

When the prophet Isaiah experienced his vision of the Lord he was overcome by his own unworthiness. "Woe is me!" he said. "For I am lost; for I am a man of unclean lips, and I dwell in the midst of a people of unclean lips; for my eyes have seen the King, the LORD of hosts!" (Isa. 6:5). In the vision an angel touched his lips with a hot coal, saying, "Behold, this has touched your lips; your guilt is taken away, and your sin forgiven" (Isa. 6:7).

"Unclean lips." We all know the times we have used our gift of speech in ways that later shame us. The Letter of James (3:2–12) singles out the tongue for this uncleanness in the lengthiest section in the Bible on human speech. It is throughout a negative commentary on our use of this ability.

> For we all make many mistakes, and if any one makes no mistakes in what he says he is a perfect man, able to bridle the whole body also. If we put bits into the mouths of horses that they may obey us, we guide their whole bodies. Look at the ships also; though they are so great and are driven by strong winds, they are guided by a very small rudder wherever the will of the pilot directs. So the tongue is a little member and boasts of great things. How great a forest is set ablaze by a small fire!
>
> And the tongue is a fire. The tongue is an unrighteous world among our members, staining the whole body, setting on fire the cycle of nature, and set on fire by hell. For every kind of beast and bird, of reptile and sea creature, can be tamed and has been tamed by

humankind, but no human being can tame the tongue—
a restless evil, full of deadly poison. With it we bless
the Lord and Father, and with it we curse men, who
are made in the likeness of God. From the same mouth
come blessing and cursing. My brethren, this ought
not to be so. Does a spring pour forth from the same
opening fresh water and brackish? Can a fig tree, my
brethren, yield olives, or a grapevine figs? No more
can salt water yield fresh.

We use the words "gossip" and "slander" to describe
a negative use of the tongue. Has anyone pictured
these activities more graphically than James in his
depiction of the tongue as a fire which sets on fire the
cycle of nature and is set on fire by hell? Or, again,
"a restless evil, full of deadly poison"?

We use the verb "tongue-lash" to describe abusive
speech. Have you ever given a tongue-lashing or received one? It is an apt description, for emotionally
we feel as though we have been lashed by repeated
blows of a whip.

There is even a term to describe saying the wrong
thing: to "put your foot in your mouth." Do you do
this? If not, do you know someone who does? Whatever the basis for this imagery of a foot in the mouth,
we know the meaning: We've said something without
thinking. It's out! It's too late to stop the words—and
it's too obvious to retract them. We say we wish we
had "bitten our tongue"—that is, halted the words by
clamping down instead on the instrument of speech.

The science of the use of words was called "rhetoric"
in former days and was regularly taught in institutions
of higher learning. Augustine was a teacher of rhetoric
before his conversion. But the word has undergone a
change in meaning, based on our disillusionment with
speech. If we use the word "rhetoric" now we usually
mean it as a pejorative. It means an ornate use of

words to cover their lack of authenticity. "It's just rhetoric," we say, meaning words, words, words, with no sincerity behind them; empty words though powerfully used, certainly not to be taken seriously.

Since George Orwell's *1984* the word "doublespeak" has become part of our vocabulary. It is a caricature of the speech of authority—especially the authority of governments—in which the normal meaning of words is completely reversed, conveying the opposite in meaning. "Saving is destroying," "lying is truth," "a war machine is a peacemaker."

Closely related to doublespeak is the double signal. "It is all right to make your own decision," we say, "but you should make the one I want you to make." Double signals are often given by authorities such as parents, who are intellectually committed to respect the space of others but emotionally want to control that space.

Silence Is Golden

Silence is golden. This familiar aphorism is an obvious put-down on speech. Why not "Speech is golden"?

But there is something to say for silence. A pioneer in the modern teaching of pastoral care, Russell Dicks, distinguished between silence and quietness. Silence can be heavy, oppressive. But quietness communicates care and security. As such, quietness is sacramental silence; that is, it communicates the presence and peace of God. Dicks called it a "ministry of presence."

This is the kind of silence that Job's three comforters gave to him in his affliction. He was in such misery physically and mentally that words seemed superfluous. So the three comforters sat with Job in quietness for seven days and seven nights. They communicated the sacramental nature of their silence by using symbols other than words to convey their compassion: they tore their robes, sprinkled dust on their heads, and wept (Job 2:12–13).

But this sacramental silence or quietness is not what is meant by "Silence is golden." Job spoke words similar to this aphorism in his frustration with his three friends—after they began to speak. Their words were so abrasive and so contrary to the spirit of their earlier quietness that Job said to them, "Oh that you would keep silent, and it would be your wisdom!" (Job 13:5).

Silence is golden when it comes as a relief from oppressive and seemingly never-ending speech. It can also be golden at those times when we are at a loss for words. What we say at these times is usually better left unsaid. Some of us can't stand silence and impulsively say something to break it, but what we say is often trite and superficial, making silence, in contrast, golden.

As somebody has noted, silence can be more yellow than golden. There are times when we *should* speak. In fact, we describe speaking on these occasions as "speaking up." These are the times when it takes courage to speak—when to remain silent would be the safer course.

Mike struggled within himself in his promotion interview because the interviewing supervisor was being unfairly critical of Mike's former boss, who had been terminated by the company. Mike knew the criticism was unjust but he also knew the interviewing supervisor was voicing the company line, which he needed to believe. Besides, Mike didn't want to jeopardize his promotion. So he said nothing.

But he felt crummy. His silence compromised his integrity. He knew he would feel uncomfortable should he ever again be in the company of his former boss. After days of inward debate, Mike finally admitted to himself and God, "I should have spoken up."

Positive Aphorisms

There is a time to speak. For this reason not all aphorisms about speech are negative. A biblical proverb says, "A word fitly spoken is like apples of gold in a setting of silver" (Prov. 25:11). A word fitly spoken makes the setting beautiful. Another proverb describes such a fitly spoken word as a "word in season" (Prov. 15:23). It comes at just the right time.

Perhaps you know people who not only know just what to say but who *say* it—and at the right time. Profiting from his long life, Benjamin Franklin said the fitting word on more than one occasion during the long hot summer months of the Constitutional Convention in 1787. Historian Catherine Drinker Bowen says of Franklin that he "was always alert to the atmosphere of a meeting" (*Miracle at Philadelphia*, p. 55; Boston: Little, Brown & Co., 1986). Through this alertness, Franklin's words may have kept the convention from disbanding in discouragement (ibid., pp. 125–127).

Winston Churchill also had this gift and at times used it acerbically. Lady Ashley was a constant critic of Churchill in the House of Commons. On one occasion in a moment of exasperation she said, "Mr. Churchill, if I were your wife I would put arsenic in your soup." Quick in riposte, Churchill responded, "And if you were my wife, madam, I would gladly eat it."

We have colloquial expressions for this gift. "He

waxed eloquent"; "She knew just what to say." Personally, I seem to think of just what to say ten minutes after the proper moment. If you also are one whose insights into what to say come in delayed fashion, you have lots of company.

2

Bodily Symbol
of Evil

As we have seen, the description of human speech in the Letter of James is as negative as most of our figures of speech about speech. Only by implied contrast is there any positive note. The only exception is the beginning sentence: "For we all make many mistakes, and if any one makes no mistakes in what he says he is a perfect man, able to bridle the whole body also" (James 3:1).

Besides being an obvious overstatement, this description of a perfect person is also an obvious impossibility, since "no human being can tame the tongue" (3:8). After this opening sentence the tongue as a symbol of human speech is for James actually a symbol of human evil.

Bodily Symbols of Human Attributes

In using a physical organ, the tongue, to represent a human or spiritual quality, James is following the Hebrew tradition of symbolizing human attributes by specific organs of the human body.

The heart is an example. Because its beats indicate both the presence and perpetuation of life, the heart is the symbol for the passions of life. Usually its use is positive, as in Isaiah 30:29: "You shall have . . . gladness of heart, as when one sets out to the sound of the flute to go to the mountain of the LORD."

But its use can also be negative, as in Jeremiah 17:9: "The heart is deceitful above all things, and desperately corrupt; who can understand it?"

Another example is the use of the abdominal area as a symbol of warmth and caring. In differentiation from the heart, the abdominal viscera represent only the tender passions of life like compassion and affection. In fact, most modern translations of the Greek word simply use the human attribute that is symbolized. When Paul writes to the Philippian congregation that he yearns for them all "with the affection of Christ Jesus" (Phil. 1:8), the Greek word for affection (*splanchna*) is actually "intestines."

This use of bodily organs to represent spiritual, mental, and emotional qualities is an expression of the holism of the Hebrew mind-set. Body, mind, and spirit are all interrelated; what affects one affects all. Our current interest in holistic health and holistic medicine is new only to our western culture.

Failures of the Tongue

In using the tongue as a symbol of human evil, James reviews the poor track record of human speech. Whereas the purpose of speech is obviously to *reveal* to others what is going on within our minds, we too often use it instead to *conceal* what is going on—to deceive. In fact we use our tongues even to deceive ourselves (James 1:26).

Instead of using our tongues to bear witness to the truth, we are equally likely to use them to bear false witness.

The tongue is an *unruly* evil. James exaggerates to make his point. "For every kind of beast and bird, of reptile and sea creature, can be tamed and has been tamed by humankind, but no human being can tame the tongue—a restless evil" (James 3:7–8).

Obviously not all animals have been tamed by human beings. Although it looks like a horse, the zebra, for example, has not been domesticated. But this is not the point. Compared to the many animals and birds and even dolphins and beluga whales that have been tamed for domestic or entertainment purposes, the human tongue stands out as untamable.

This use of hyperbole is typical of the diatribal style in which this letter is written. Characteristic of this writing format, popular in his day, James in his letter makes his comparisons and conclusions simplistic to catch his reader's attention.

Consonant with Other Scripture

This exaggerated description of the powers of the tongue is not peculiar to James. Similar assertions are found throughout the Bible, particularly in the Wisdom literature of the Old Testament, which is probably a source for James. The Book of Proverbs has several such claims. "He who guards his mouth preserves his life" (13:3). Or, again "He who keeps his mouth and his tongue keeps himself out of trouble" (21:23).

In the New Testament, the First Letter of Peter quotes from Psalm 34: "He that would love life and see good days, let him keep his tongue from evil and his lips from speaking guile" (1 Peter 3:10; cf. Ps. 34:13).

Paul in his Letter to the Romans quotes Psalm 5: "Their throat is an open grave, they use their tongues

to deceive. The venom of asps is under their lips"
(Rom. 3:13; cf. Ps. 5:9). The last description is similar
to James's depiction of the tongue as "full of deadly
poison" (James 3:8).

The Letter to Titus condemns "empty talkers" (1:10).
This judgment is similar to that of Jesus on "careless"
words. "For by your words you will be justified, and
by your words you will be condemned" (Matt. 12:37).

I know from experience this judgment on careless
words. When I reach a stage of euphoria my tongue
seems to lose its connection with my common sense.
I become less sensitive to the sensitivities of others,
and careless words slip out easily and quickly.

Would we really be completely fulfilled if we had
perfect control over our tongues? These references to
the tongue, mouth, and lips from both Testaments
would lead us to think so. They are hyperboles of the
tongue's representation of the human spirit. Our words
are also more than symbols, they are actual behavior—
our conduct.

Speaking on Impulse

The negative use of the tongue is often due to
speaking on impulse. This is because the impulse is
often motivated by irritation, annoyance, or outrage.
We are pushed passed the toleration point, and we
let fly with our words.

Child care authority Rudolf Dreikurs cautioned parents against speaking on impulse with their children.
"It is essential," he said, "to avoid the first impulse.
Instead, stop and consider" (*Children: The Challenge*,
p. 181; New York: Hawthorne Books, 1964). This is
the time to retire to the bathroom and close the door.

Dreikurs then explained why the child usually does

not understand the reason for the misbehavior or disturbance. "Often neither he nor his parents are aware that it is a part of his attempt to find a place and to belong to the group. If his behavior violates order and disrupts cooperation, he is using faulty methods to reach his basic goal, and an impulsive response usually reinforces his mistaken assumption" (p. 186).

As an example, Dreikurs went on to describe a family scene most parents can identify with. Daddy and his three children were building a snowman together. The oldest child, age eight, lost interest in the project and developed a game of his own of running and then sliding in the snow. First he slid into the snowman, knocking off its head. "Watch it," Daddy said crossly as the boy insisted he didn't mean to do it. Next the boy slid into his sister, age six, knocking her, howling, into the snowman.

This was too much for Daddy. "Bevin, go into the house," he said with restrained intensity. "We'd rather not have you out here" (p. 182).

Bevin, Dreikurs explained, had been twice dethroned by his younger sisters and no longer believed he had a place in the family. His disruptive behavior was an unconscious attempt to test out his belief, and he managed to get himself rejected. "If Daddy had understood Bevin's doubt about having a place in the family and knew why he prompted rejection, he could have avoided that first impulse to send Bevin away" (p. 187).

But if your parental understanding is like mine, it may not be working that well when a child misbehaves. We may find it more helpful simply to adopt as our principle not to speak on impulse. The few times we may speak constructively on impulse are not worth the many times we will speak destructively.

Impulse vs. Spontaneity

Speaking on impulse is frequently confused with spontaneity. Yet an impulse is not the same as a spontaneous desire. "Spontaneity" comes from the root *sponte,* meaning "free will" or natural, congruent or whole. When we speak spontaneously we are speaking out of wholeness. The words are congruent with our congruent self. They express our inner unity.

Congruent and whole are precisely what we are *not* when we speak on impulse. While it looks like spontaneity in that we are not guarded or concerned about how we may sound, speaking on impulse actually comes from inner division—a *disunity.*

"Impulse" is related to the verb "impel," which means to push or force. When we speak on impulse our words are literally impelled out of our mouths by an inner force that has temporarily blocked our discerning mind.

When we speak impulsively—to a child or a spouse or even to a friend who is annoying us—our disapproval of such speaking has been overcome by the intensity of our reaction to the annoyance.

There is probably a latent resistance within us to listen to our discerning mind when people annoy us. Part of us would like to turn loose our tongues and "let them have it." But this part is held in check by wiser reflection. When the negative stimulus reaches a certain intensity, this latent resistance ceases to be latent. In the internal insurrection that follows, control of the tongue is abandoned.

It is as though we had a child within us who is controlled by the parent within us. When the parent is not looking, the child makes a forbidden move, hoping to be back in place by the time the parent glances back. But like all children the child within us is ready to give a quick defense or rationalization of this bad behavior if it isn't done quickly enough to avoid detection.

Another way of conceptualizing the insurrection is to think of our having both an acceptable self and an unacceptable self. Normally the acceptable self keeps the unacceptable self in check. But when external pressures mount, the unacceptable self sees the opportunity to get in a fast jab—or make a quick end run—while the acceptable self is immobilized by the stress of the moment.

We can imagine that Daddy in Dreikurs's story was anticipating a good time with his children in making that snowman. This, after all, was to be family fun. It was his time with the children. He probably was subliminally aware that Bevin might act up. Yet he had no conscious intention of ejecting Bevin from the scene.

But when he saw the snowman collapsing for the second time with the screams of his daughter piercing his ears, it was more than even good intentions could cope with.

The Slow Progression to Guilt

Daddy probably defended his impulsive words as he and the girls set about to repair the snowman. After all, Bevin asked for it! If he can't behave and cooperate he doesn't belong out here. Daddy felt supported by what he discerned as his daughters' agreement.

But Daddy also knew that after a while his anger would abate and in its place would come guilt. Later, as he related the incident to his wife, he was still half defending himself. Finally, however, his defenses collapsed. "I just wish I hadn't said it," he confessed. His wife was understanding. In fact she understood all too well.

When I speak on impulse, my hard side comes out. It is only recently that a close confidant shared this observation of my behavior. When I am resisted or challenged—whether by my children, spouse, or colleagues—I push hard, impulsively, to overcome this resistance.

This behavior is an integral part of a defensive-offensive syndrome. When I feel challenged I strike out verbally. It is my instinctive, habitual reaction to those who resist my way of seeing things.

I have found that by giving this tendency of my tongue a name, I am in a better position to control it. I do not wish to use my tongue to attack a child, spouse, or colleague—even if I believe, often distortedly, that they have attacked *me*. This is the first step toward achieving the freedom I desire in order to direct my tongue.

The Need for a Bridle

James describes this desire for freedom to direct our tongues as the need for a bridle. For bridling the tongue means bridling the whole body, or controlling our total behavior. This is why we put bits into the mouths of beasts—"that they may obey us" and we may "guide their whole bodies" (James 3:3). The bridle then is the symbol for control—for freedom.

And it is our faith in God that can give us this freedom. James states it conversely: "If anyone thinks he is religious, and does not bridle his tongue but deceives his heart, this person's religion is vain" (1:26).

So while the tongue may never be fully tamed—it can be bridled!

3

Symbol of Communication—
Or Its Failure?

Speech is not the only way in which we humans communicate. There are wide ranges of nonverbal communications, particularly in intimate circles like the family.

You can tell—by the way your father narrows his eyes, or your wife drops her glance, or your husband becomes quiet, or your child grows uninterested in a family activity—that something is bothering them. You've lived with your family members long enough to recognize their nonverbal signals, and they, yours. Some of us twitch, others become restless, and still others put on a long face. The old expression said it well: a face that would stop a clock.

Words Safeguard Nonverbal Communication

But you can also read these nonverbal signals wrongly. Think of the times when someone, even in the family, got the wrong impression from *you*. Perhaps they thought you were displeased by something they said because of the expression on your face while they were speaking. Actually your mind had wandered to an unrelated disturbing memory as they spoke. But they thought you were listening intently to *them*.

Obviously the clearest way to communicate is with words.

It is also the safest way. It is precisely for this reason that in this nuclear age we have a hot line to Moscow. This phone line supposedly is always open (although it has been known to be out of order), so that the leaders of either country can quickly converse. Should either nation receive a nonverbal signal from the other that is threatening in nature, the tongues can get going to clarify the communication. Since both leaders have only fifteen to twenty minutes to decide what to do if they believe the other is launching a nuclear attack, it is imperative immediately to engage the chief form of communication.

The leading U.S. negotiator in securing the release of the fifty-two American hostages from our embassy in Iran early in 1981 was Warren Christopher. He was the capable Deputy Secretary of State who became almost a nightly source of news during that tense period.

Speaking from experience, Christopher lauded the role of the tongue in the family of nations. "Talking receives less attention than it deserves," he said; it is a "central element in our foreign relations."

Concerned about the hardening line nations are taking toward each other when they are in conflict, Christopher warned, "We may come to think we can punish our adversaries by refusing to talk—or, by our silence, induce changes in policies we deplore. But without talking, without diplomacy, an essential ingredient of our national security is lost" (*Parade* magazine).

Symbol of the Failure of Communication

But the tongue too can fail. In fact James considers it a symbol for the failure of communication rather than a symbol of communication. While the tongue is needed to prevent strife among nations, it is often the stimulus for strife within the family.

Family intimacy depends on each family member's keeping the others informed of what is going on. This helps each to know the other. Yet in our families we too often use our tongues to give the opposite impression from our actual state of mind.

We choose to hide behind our words, for in hiding we are secured against being known. There is safety in concealment. Why? Because we believe that if we are intimate with another—and the other really knows us—he or she may hurt us, probably by rejecting us.

Our illusion that concealment provides security often extends to our nonverbal communication. Some of us are so good at giving misleading nonverbal communication that even family members are fooled. We even look as though we are feeling OK when we are not.

Others, in contrast, "wear their feelings on their sleeve." They may deny their obvious nonverbal communication if they are asked about it. Yet their words lack the feeling tone needed to convince. "What's wrong?" we ask the silent and crestfallen one. "Nothing," is the reply, but the word lacks conviction.

Besides using our tongue to give misleading impressions that frustrate family intimacy, we can frustrate it even further by using our tongue to berate rather than to prize one another. We cut others down rather than build them up. We discourage rather than encourage them.

This critical use of the tongue exacerbates family conflict and initiates a state of war. Power struggles are set in motion as the combatants take to the offense to defend themselves against verbal attack.

This negative use of words destroys more than family intimacy; it also destroys *persons*. The verbal attacks diminish our self-esteem. Our confidence goes out the back door. Our sense of worth slithers to the bottom. Even though we defend ourselves, we grow to believe the judgment leveled against us. The attack comes from those too significant in our lives not to be taken seriously.

Restoring Communication

When families get locked into this destructive use of the tongue they often need someone from outside to help them reverse the downward spiral. In marriage and family counseling the goal is to restore communication to its basic purpose: namely, a means for knowing one another.

If we think of family relationships as systems of communication, then the counselor's task is to unplug the system which has been clogged by the negative use of the tongue, so that the channels are cleared for positive communication.

If we think of the destructive use of the tongue as being counterproductive to the establishment of intimacy, then the counselor's task is to assist family members to use their power of speech productively. When this happens, the story of the family's functioning will change.

A married couple coming to a counselor tend to talk each to the counselor even though they are seated side by side. Since the counselor's task is to facilitate their talking together, he or she may have to interrupt this tendency.

After Hank and Martha had been talking to me about each other for half an hour I decided the time had come for this needed interruption. As Hank related how *she* cut him down when he didn't live up to *her* expectations, I asked, "Hank, who is *she*?"

Pointing sideways at his wife rather than looking at her, he said, "Martha, of course."

"Well," I said, "she is sitting right beside you. Why not tell *her*?"

"Tell her what?" he asked.

"Tell her what you just told me about her," I said.

"Now?" he asked.

"Yes," I said. "Now."

Hank slowly turned his neck as though there were a crow bar stiffening it. (We usually resist looking at the person we are angry with.) He told her. As he anticipated, she didn't like it. He reacted by telling her that he didn't like the way she said she didn't like it. She warmed to the occasion by telling him he didn't deserve to be told any differently.

By this time they were doing what they didn't want to do—quarreling in front of the pastor.

While the couple may find this embarrassing, since few of us quarrel with much grace, the argument nevertheless gives the counselor the opportunity to see the relationship in action. It is not the most complimentary way to see it, but it is realistic.

Martha could have described their relationship to me, and so could Hank—but with their highly subjective interpretations, I would not have gotten the picture I saw when they quarreled.

Because of this possibility of quarreling, I find it helpful as a counselor to sit between the couple and the door. While I've never had a woman try to bolt, I have had several men make the attempt.

The nonverbal communication usually tells me when the move is coming. The manly fist pounds on something, usually the palm of the other hand, and with the words "I won't hear any more of this," the man heads for the door.

This is the only time I resort to the macho image of male. I quickly rise to meet him and say, "Oh, come now, you're no chicken. You can take it." This normally works. I said it once to a marine sergeant, however, and instead of grudgingly returning to his seat, he decked me before striding out.

While the counselor learns a lot about the marital relationship by observing the couple as they quarrel, he or she can also assist in the quarrel. If I can stop one of the partners before they let go at the other, I will say, to the husband, for example, "Before you answer, will you tell me what she said?"

Looking a bit discomfited at being stopped in the heat of battle, the husband will make an attempt to repeat his wife's words. Then I'll ask the wife, "Is this what you said?" Nine times out of ten, the reply is, "It is not!"

"No? Then what *did* you say?" She will then say it again.

The husband in turn looks a little nonplussed. "Is that what she said before?" he asks.

"It's what I believe I heard," I answer.

"Well," he replies, "then that's different."

The fact is that we do not hear well when our emotions rise in a quarrel. Instead we read many past remembrances into what is said by the other and "hear" in terms of these remembrances. Also, we are so anxious to reenter the fray when the other is talking that we may cease to listen altogether in our determination to set the record straight.

If in our family quarrels we can pause sufficiently to restate what we believe is the other's point, we not only make clarification possible where probably much is needed, we also interrupt the impulsive reactions long enough for some semblance of reason to appear.

Besides, even when we are angry it is a positive experience to receive the evidence that we have been understood—or at least that the other has made the attempt and is open for correction.

"Take with You Words"

The failure to use words for communication accounts for much misunderstanding in families. Carol had had an important job for several years before she had a baby. She then chose to become a full-time home-maker, having, in her words, "had enough of the world out there."

Sam was deeply engrossed in his job and was making sufficient money to support the new family. But Carol didn't realize how much she would now be dependent on Sam to supply the affirmation she had previously received from her job. Nor did Sam.

Carol's unanticipated discontent erupted into the marriage, and together they sought counseling.

Since Carol had taken the responsibility for making the appointment, she began by making a typical over-statement that laid the blame on Sam. "The plain fact is, Sam doesn't do or say anything to show appreciation for me or for what I do."

I looked at Sam. "That's not true," he said.

"Oh, no?" Carol said. "Prove it." I concurred.

"That's easy," Sam said. "Take yesterday."

"Yesterday?" Carol said incredulously. "What did you do or say yesterday that showed any appreciation for me?"

"For your information," Sam shot back, "I came home for lunch!"

"You came home for lunch!" she exclaimed, looking

at me. "Well, big deal! That just meant I had to fix him something to eat."

Sam looked disgusted as he also looked at me. "You see how it is? You just can't talk to her anymore."

"Wait a minute," I said. "I think you just *did*. Sam, were you saying that you came home for lunch because you wanted to be with Carol?"

"Of course," he said. "Why else?"

I looked at Carol and knew what was coming. "Well, why didn't you say so!"

Being a man I knew Sam's reply. "Why do I have to say so?"

"Sam," I said, "aren't you being a bit dense? You have the answer right in front of you. You need to say so because Carol obviously didn't get it."

Nonverbal communications of caring—like Sam's coming home for lunch—expand our family communication. But because they can be misread or even misunderstood, they need to be labeled with words. The verbal then clarifies the nonverbal, allowing the nonverbal to enrich the verbal.

"Sam," I said. "Tell Carol now."

"Tell her what?" he asked.

"What you just told me. Say, 'Carol, I came home for lunch yesterday because I wanted to be with you.'"

"Do I have to?" Sam showed his resistance nonverbally as well.

"Is it the truth?" I asked.

"Yes," he said.

"Then what have you against speaking the truth?"

When he said it, I asked Carol how it felt to hear it. "Good," she said, "real good."

Sam can give Carol the reinforcement she needs by learning to put words to his positive feelings toward her. As the prophet Hosea said, "Take with you words" (Hos. 14:2).

God's Family Communication

Our relationship to God is described in both Testaments by family images. God is called our Parent and also our Spouse. In these family-like relationships God communicates with us through Word and Sacrament.

The Word of God we understand as words. In written form the Word is our Bible. Our use of the Letter of James is an example of using the Word.

The sacraments are comparable to the nonverbal communication in these intimate relationships. The Sacrament of Holy Communion will serve as an illustration. This rite provides us with a dramatic participation in a family meal. As communicants we take with us at this table the bread which conveys the body of Christ and the cup which conveys the blood of Christ. In receiving this bread and wine or grape juice into our digestive tract we are in effect receiving Christ's redemptive sacrifice into the deep recesses of our spirit. We are communing with Christ through this powerful participation in his forgiving love.

All churches of which I am aware use the rubric of the words of institution to celebrate this sacrament, words such as, "Take, eat, this is my body which is given for you. . . . Drink, all of you; this is the cup of the new covenant in my blood, which is shed for you for the forgiveness of sin." Why? Obviously to label what is being dramatized. Think of the confusion that might have occurred through the centuries if these words were not used to clarify this rite.

In our communication with God as with the family analogues, the nonverbal (the Sacrament) enhances the verbal (the Word), and the verbal clarifies the nonverbal—for the enrichment of communication.

4

Bridle for the Tongue

A governing principle for the tongue given by James at the beginning of his letter could serve as the very bridle he says the tongue requires. "Know this, my beloved brethren. Let every one of you be quick to hear, slow to speak, slow to anger" (1:19). One "quick" and two "slow"s. By beginning with the imperative "Know this," or "Remember this," or "Commit this to memory," James stresses to his readers the importance of what is to follow.

Familiar Old Covenant Wisdom Sayings

These directives within this principle are familiar Old Covenant wisdom sayings which James puts together in this triad. For example, Proverbs 16:32: "He who is slow to anger is better than the mighty"; and Proverbs 14:29: "He who is slow to anger has great understanding"; and 10:19: "When words are many, transgression is not lacking, but he who restrains his lips is prudent."

The apocryphal Wisdom book of Ecclesiasticus has similar directives. "Be quick to listen, and deliberate in giving an answer. . . . If you love listening you will learn, if you lend an ear, wisdom will be yours. . . . A wise [person] will keep quiet till the right moment,

but a garrulous fool will always misjudge it" (Ecclus.
5:11; 6:33; 20:7, JB).

Quick to Listen

We are well aware that it may take courage at times
to speak. Yet we are probably not as aware that it may
take just as much courage at other times to listen. At
these times we may speak impulsively simply to keep
control of the conversation or to relieve our own tension or to live up to a fancied expectation that we
know what to say.

Husbands, for example, often have a difficult time
listening to their wives when they express their concerns. Instead, they feel the tension to provide answers
to quiet the concern. Do husbands feel responsible
for their wives' contentment? Or obligated to be the
strong one in the marriage?

But of course wives also may need courage to listen
to their husbands. When we listen we may think we
know what the other will say, but we can never be
sure. This element of the unknown is, subliminally at
least, a threat to our control over things, particularly
when we are bonded to the other. We can walk away
from the uncomfortable words of a stranger or even
of an acquaintance, but it is an illusion to think we
can do the same with a family member.

Slow to Speak

Being slow to speak means seeing to it that our
speaking does not get in the way of our listening. "If
one gives answer before he hears, it is his folly and
shame" (Prov. 18:13). Yet it is common for us to come

in with answers or even with rebuttals before we have really understood the question or the substance of the other's position.

The first principle of good counseling, for example, is to listen not only to the rational content of the counselee's communication but also to the feeling tone of that communication. As a teacher of counseling I find this one of my most difficult challenges, since it seems to be unnatural in our culture to listen to the full communication of others—particularly their feelings.

Rather than letting our tongue get in the way of our listening, which it is inclined to do, we should direct it to draw out the communication of the other—to assist them in their speaking.

An incident on a family trip stands out in my memory. It was the last of our family vacations when most of our children still went along. We had been deep-sea fishing off the coast of Maine and, in returning, stopped off in Boston to see my old haunts as a student there years before. I recognized the cafeteria where I had worked as a busboy. "Let's have breakfast there," I said, "I'd like to see it again."

As soon as we were inside I saw the difference. Urban blight had taken its toll. A group of people were standing at what was evidently a food counter. As I was trying to get my bearings a voice called from behind the counter, "Get in line if you want to eat!"

As we took our place in line I could feel my interest in this restaurant slipping away. When we reached the man with the voice, he asked, "What do you want?"

"Orange juice," I said.

"Don't have any," he said with sadistic pleasure.

"Well, what *do* you have?" I asked.

"Grapefruit juice," he said.

"Fine," I replied. He discovered that the grapefruit juice was downstairs. With audible cursing he went to get it.

When he returned with the grapefruit juice he nicked himself with the can opener in his haste to dispense with us—and this was followed by even more audible curses. The implication of all this was that it was my fault.

By this time every parent knows what I was about to hear. "What did you bring us in *here* for?" I was wondering the same thing. We were at the final stage of a good vacation and looking forward to getting back to familiar surroundings and friends. How could I have better used my tongue to draw something other than inner-city cynicism from this man? I hated to see this comedown in family spirit.

Then it dawned on me that I had received too much change. The man had forgotten to charge us for our beverages. I had a brilliant idea. Perhaps I could still redeem the situation and provide a valuable lesson for the kids at the same time.

"Let's go back up to the counter," I said to the child feeling most rejected by the situation. "I have an idea."

"I'm not going back there again," she said.

"Trust me—just this once," I pleaded.

So we went up. "What now?" he said in his strident voice.

"Sir," I said, "I don't believe you charged us for our drinks."

"Mm." He frowned. "Let's check it." After refiguring the bill he said, "You're right."

"Here you are," I said, handing the extra money to him. For the first time a smile cracked that frozen face. "Thanks," he said, "thanks a lot." But that isn't all. When he smiled, instead of his lips curving upward, they curved downward.

When we returned to our table the others noticed the difference in our spirits. "What happened to you?" they asked. And so we told them. By then we were all feeling better.

I probably would have forgotten the incident except that this same child said to me a month or so later, "Dad, do you remember that man in the restaurant in Boston?"

"I surely do," I said.

"Well, that new neighbor who moved in up the street reminds me of him."

"How is that?" I asked.

"Each morning on my way to school he is often out doing yard work. When I say 'Hi,' he never looks at me but just grunts. This morning I remembered the man in Boston. So I thought, I'm going to try something. So after the grunt I just stood there. Finally he realized I was there and looked up. I smiled and said 'Hi' again. For the first time he smiled. And believe it or not, Dad, when he smiled he smiled downward."

In both instances we had used our tongues to draw out the better nature of people who seem to meet the world with suspicion. And when this happens everyone feels better.

The same is true when we use our tongue as an aid to our listening. It is anything but encouraging if the one to whom we are speaking shows only a minimal interest in what we are saying. In this case, silence discourages listening, and perfunctory comments do little better. Yet if we show *verbally* that we have been following what the other has been saying, we are encouraging the other to continue. If we also ask questions that not only show we are interested but also help the other to clarify what he or she is saying, we help the other to feel good about communicating. This in turn helps them to feel better about themselves—and, not incidentally, about us.

The common complaint of family members about their family communication is the lack of listening. It seems not to dawn on the complainer that he or she is also probably guilty of this same lack. Children say either to or about their parents, "You—they—never listen!" Spouse says to spouse, "You don't hear me!" And parents say to children, "You don't pay any attention to what I say!"

Even when we parents say *no* to our children, the way in which we say it affects the children's feelings— about us, about themselves, and about the issue at hand. Few of us like to say *no* to our children. I know I didn't. But we often need to do so. This is one reason why children need parents; they lack the maturity to decide wisely for themselves. So they need the protection of parental decision.

Nor can we expect children to accept a *no* with equanimity. Rather, they resent it. Yet if we have heard them out in their reasons and feelings, and show them we understand where they are coming from, even though we cannot concur, they can take the *no* better. They still don't like it—but the relationship is less negatively affected.

Threatened by What We Hear

Being quick to listen is particularly difficult when we are threatened by what we hear—which is always a possibility in family living. Who likes to hear a child's objection to our suggestion, or even direction? They do not want to eat their vegetables, and we know they need vegetables for their health. Why are their palates so differently conditioned from ours? Or are they as yet unconditioned?

These conflicts over the immediate likes and dislikes of our children take on a profounder significance in adolescence when the differences are over personal values, religious beliefs and traditions, and moral principles.

As children mature they have a need to be independent. One way they seek to meet this need is by taking different positions from their parents on values. This runs counter to the parents' need to have their children hold to the same values.

Though they may not voice it, parents fear their children may veer away from what they have taught them.

In older days when parental control was assumed, we asked, "Would you permit your daughter"—always the daughter—"to marry a Catholic—[or a Protestant]?" Later it became a Negro (or a white). Now we raise the more relevant question, "How would you take it if they *did*?"

The big fear of religious parents is that their children may not follow the religion in which they were reared. And the same fear must also exist for those parents who are opposed to religion. And it can happen either way.

Although Bill Murray was the child on whose behalf the well-known atheist crusader Madalyn Murray O'-Hair filed her historic suit against religion in the public schools, he not only forsook the atheism of his mother as he grew up but became an evangelical Christian preacher.

What we parents fear, of course, is our loss of control over our children. If a parent has relied on physical force to ensure conformity, what happens when children get too big to force? When they are recognized as adults in our society and therefore free of parental control, what then?

It is only to be expected that we would want our children to hold to the moral and religious beliefs and values we believe are right and true. But it can also be embarrassing should they deviate from these values. What will those in our larger family think— brothers, sisters, parents, cousins, neighbors, fellow church members? Do they see this deviance as a reflection on the parents?

These possibilities regarding our children are a risk that all who become parents take. But it is often unfaced. Probably it is just as well. If we took any of these possibilities with the seriousness of later parenthood, we might back away from the challenge. And it is a challenge that one needs to grow *into*, both emotionally and intellectually, as parents themselves can change within the actual context of the challenge.

Usually we do not like to listen to people with political, religious, economic, and moral views different from our own. We veer away from them and choose people of similar views as our friends. But it is hard at times to know. What host has not had the experience of guests getting into tense moments of disagreement on these issues?

When James Boswell took his esteemed friend Samuel Johnson to visit his parents, the sparks soon flew between Johnson and Boswell's father, who differed vehemently in politics and religion. Boswell describes the pain of being caught in the middle.

> They became exceedingly warm, and violent, and I was very much distressed by being present at such an altercation between two men, both of whom I reverenced, yet I durst not interfere. It would certainly be very unbecoming in me to exhibit my honored father, and my respected friend, as intellectual gladiators, for

the entertainment of the publick, and therefore I suppress what would, I dare say, make an interesting scene in this dramatick sketch. (Quoted in Ian Ousby, *Literary Britain and Ireland*, p. 280; New York: W. W. Norton & Co., 1985)

This dislike of differences intensifies immensely when such views are expressed by our children. Some of my students on occasion have shared with me their reluctance to go either to their parents' home or the home of their in-laws for vacation periods. The problem—differences in values that neither can seemingly handle.

"We've learned to confine ourselves to two subjects," one young man said, "the weather and what's been going on around the home place. But how long does it take before these subjects have run their course? We don't agree on religion, on politics, on morality, or economics, and whenever we get into these areas we end up in a quarrel no one feels good about."

This is lamentable. I find differences as threatening as most people, but I don't want my children to be reluctant to share where they are with me because of my inability to listen. I suspect that the student's parents and in-laws feel as he does. As in so many intergenerational gatherings, these parents and their children have learned how to keep the conversation safe by keeping it superficial. They sacrifice the potential joy of intimacy for a thin and tenuous harmony.

When this happens we parents forfeit the opportunity of becoming friends with our adult children, and we children forfeit the opportunity of becoming friends with our parents and in-laws. The threat of difference opens us to another threat, the threat that we cannot control—bridle—our tongues.

It is hard for parents to let children go if they are not going in the direction we had in mind for them.

We then withhold in some sense our parental blessing. It is also difficult for children to learn unless we differentiate ourselves in some way from our parents. Otherwise we spend our lives defending our parents rather than facing our differences.

How different it is when we can listen to what we don't want to hear. We can then risk the possibility of dialogue in which we as well as the others may be influenced to change.

Maybe this is what we fear: that our own position is not as secure as we might hope. The very nature of dialogue—of listening and speaking with mutual respect—exposes us to the unpredictable. Again we are faced with the possible loss of control. So we back off—becoming, instead, slow to listen and quick to interrupt with our own speaking—to set the other straight before he or she shakes our foundations. As tempers rile, tongues get going so fast that our ears don't function, even though we have two of them.

Here is where "slow to anger" is needed to complete the bridle.

5

Anger:
A Precarious Passion

Anger is a natural human passion. Without it we would not be fully human. Since we are created in the image of God, anger is a reflection of the divine in us, for God has anger.

Reaction to Injustice

Anger is primarily a reaction to injustice. The biblical prophets' anger against those who oppress their fellow human beings is the classical example. The following from the prophet Amos (5:11–12) is typical:

> Therefore because you trample upon the poor
>   and take from him exactions of wheat,
> you have built houses of hewn stone,
>   but you shall not dwell in them;
> you have planted pleasant vineyards,
>   but you shall not drink their wine.
> For I know how many are your transgressions,
>   and how great are your sins—
> you who afflict the righteous, who take a bribe,
>   and turn aside the needy in the gate.

This oppression continues today. It is behind the conflicts that are racking Central America. It is behind the impoverishment of much of Africa.

This oppression also is against those who want to reform this injustice. Again Amos: "They hate him who reproves in the gate, and they abhor him who speaks the truth" (5:10). If anything, this oppression against those who protest against injustice is even worse today than ever. Scores of nations in this world regularly imprison, torture, and kill those who dare object to the powers that be.

Whenever I receive *Amnesty Action*, the bimonthly newsletter of the United States Section of Amnesty International, and read therein the accounts of torture of these contemporary prisoners of conscience, I feel depressed. A better response, however, would be anger.

The same is true in regard to what appears to be an epidemic of child abuse, spouse abuse, and the abuse of the elderly in our midst. We need more anger, not less, over these attacks upon the poor and vulnerable and defenseless in our midst.

Yet James says that "the anger of man does not work the righteousness of God" (1:20). Again we are dealing with hyperbole. Certainly *much* expression of human anger is not constructive. Rather, in most instances this anger leads to various degrees of *destructive* behavior, including our use of speech.

Our human anger tends to be destructive because it gets mixed up with our human egocentricity. We are more likely to be concerned about injustice against *me* or *my* family or *my* community or *my* church or *my* country. The farther away the injustice occurs, the less concerned we tend to be.

Even worse, we become oblivious of our own involvement in these faraway injustices. A prime example is our general indifference to our own government's role over the years in supporting oppressive regimes in third world nations, particularly in our own hemisphere, ostensibly to protect our national and business interests in these unfortunate nations.

A Secondary Passion

Anger is also a secondary passion; that is, it is a reaction to more primal passions. It is as a secondary passion that anger is most likely to erupt within the family.

This anger is frequently a reaction to the passion of fear. This is particularly true of males, since males in our society have difficulty expressing their fear lest they appear weak and thereby invite attack from other males. From the school playground to the marketplace to the decision-making bodies of the churches, men tend to hide their fear behind a macho exterior.

Women also may find their most protective expression of their fear through their anger. All of us—male and female, old and young—have been influenced by the adage of the coaches that the best defense in any threatening situation is a good offense. When scared—attack! And usually this means, at least in the beginning, verbal attack.

Anger is also a reaction to guilt. Like fear, the passion of guilt is uncomfortable, even painful. In reaction to this pain we tend to attack whoever seems to be stimulating our guilt.

Some people are particularly good at guilt-tripping. Others stimulate guilt within us simply because their behavior reflects uncomfortably on our own. They make us angry simply because they are good. Rather than confessing our guilt or changing our behavior, we may instead lash out at the one we feel is directly or indirectly responsible for our discomfort of guilt.

Anger is also a reaction to hurt feelings. These feelings abound in family living. Children often feel hurt by what seems to be a parent's favoring another sibling. But they show it in angry charges. "You always let *him* have his way!" "You never listen to me, just to *her*!"

Hurt feelings are basically feelings of being rejected. Not only are they painful—which is sufficient in itself to make us angry—they imply an attack on us by the other. There is no greater spiritual pain than that of rejection. So we retaliate by anger—even hate.

Physical pain is also a stimulus to anger. If you should bump your shin or nick your finger, isn't any family member who happens to be nearby in a geographically precarious position? Even if they only breathe, you may seize on this as a reason for an attack. If they succeed in remaining absolutely motionless, you may still lash out in your discomfort with the familiar denunciation, "Well, don't just stand there!" What does this mean? Obviously it makes no rational sense to say it. But it doesn't have to be rational, because our pain is primarily emotional. We hurt, and this makes us angry, and we need someone to dump our anger on.

Anger as Frustration

Another generator of anger is frustration. Frustration also is a discomfort, a pain, and as such is usually expressed by anger. Frustration is a buildup of tension due to obstacles in the way to the fulfillment of our goals. It frustrates us to feel powerless before these obstacles. They are blocks to the satisfaction of our desires and exert severe restraints on our freedom. We rage within at being so powerless without.

Parents may encounter such frustrations at work. Children experience them at school or in the neighborhood. In both instances these frustrations focus on our relationships. *Things* are difficult to deal with at times, but people are worse.

Because we don't seem to deal with these frustrations where they originate, we tend to bring them home with us. Our family relationships are usually less tenuous than those in the workplace, at school, or in the neighborhood.

Our anger needs a target, and family members are the most likely candidates. In the family we are bonded by a love that is the nearest to the love of God that we know. It is not limited like the relationships we have at work or at school.

So family members are safer objects upon whom to vent our frustrations. It is as though we are saying, You're family. You've got to take it since others won't.

In fact, it can be frightening if a family member refuses to take it. We are counting on their love being unconditional—so we may exploit it for our own needs. This is the common human need for a scapegoat to relieve us of the pains of our frustration.

Would you not think that we scapegoaters would have compassion for the family member on whom we are dumping? But in the strange logic of scapegoating, we evade this compassion by convincing ourselves that the other is the proper recipient for what we are getting rid of. He or she *deserves* it!

What is the effect upon the one who is *being* scapegoated in the family? Does it help you, for example, to know that you are simply the safe and convenient target for anger generated elsewhere? That the dumping is really not personal? Do you see yourself as helping the other by taking their pains upon yourself so that the frustration does not escalate within them into self-destructive proportions? Probably not. The attack hurts too much not to take it seriously—even personally.

The need for a scapegoat can extend beyond temporary frustrations at work or school. Life itself can seem unfair. By implication the God of the universe is uncaring.

But it is hard to attack life or God, even though the pain we believe they are causing makes us angry and perhaps even bitter. We need something more concrete and tangible than *life,* and something more tangible and safe than God. Again, the family may appear to fill this need. We may scapegoat family members with anger that is really intended for God—and even scapegoat ourselves rather than take on the Almighty.

Abusive and Arrogant

When anger is verbally expressed in families it comes out in abusive and arrogant ways. The angry one arrogates to himself or herself the position of judge. The object of the anger is abused in verbal put-downs and with uncharitable labels. The angry one is on top, passing judgments on the other beneath.

In such verbal judging there is usually an increase in the volume with which it is pronounced. In fact, we can be nose to nose and still shout. The other may protest, "Why are you shouting? Do you think I'm deaf?" To which we may instinctively shout "Yes!" By this we mean, You have been deaf to my normal voice. You haven't heard me.

The increased volume of anger often intimidates its recipient. This is one reason we may let ourselves become angry. This is a battle we want to win. One thing is certain, however: shouting gets a hearing. Perhaps this also is its purpose.

Another tactic in our verbal attacks in the family is exaggeration. Instead of saying, "You often do that," we say, "You *always* do that!" Instead of, "Occasionally you don't," it is, "You *never* do!" This also gets a hearing. Telling it like it is hasn't worked. So turn up the intensity of the story and exaggerate.

But instead of capitulating or repenting before our verbal onslaught, the other usually finds our style contagious. So for our increase in volume, we get a returned increase from the other. For our exaggerations, we are bombarded in return by the exaggerated accusations of the other. The one is offense and the other defense, yet you can scarcely determine the difference by the volume and by the stretch in the truth.

So it is charge, countercharge, supercharge, supercountercharge, until we reach the escalation of uproar. The verbal bombast is the sign that our normal communication has broken down. These extremes in verbal exchange are really a desperate attempt to communicate when communication has ceased. And we *do* communicate—albeit usually destructively. Yet the underlying purpose of the quarrel is to restore normal—constructive—communication.

If we could stay with the quarreling without becoming physically violent, we probably could move into a more rational communication and be on our way to achieve a constructive interchange. After all, there is a limit to the amount of volume and the extremity of exaggeration that either can generate, and sooner or later we exhaust not only our repertoire of weapons but also ourselves. Then the quarrel will have served its purpose. We might even say, in retrospect, I don't like to be shouted at, but I guess I have not been hearing you and I'm grateful for the breakthrough.

The Silent Treatment

There is another destructive climax to quarreling, in addition to physical violence: namely, silence. Somebody gives a final outburst—"I'll not hear any more of this!"—and out they go, slamming doors and leaving the house shaking with the impact.

After this there is quiet—but it is a painful quiet, an oppressive quiet. Becoming quiet has become a substitute for the quarrel rather than a follow-up. This is not the "slow to speak" to which James refers as a bridle for the tongue—the "slow to speak" that is an aid to being "quick to listen." In fact, in this silence there is an actual resistance to listening. If we can reasonably get away with the pretense, we may act as though we had not heard the other, even when we have.

This is the silent treatment. The silence, of course, may not be total. We may give short, terse answers when it is obvious that we have heard the other: "Yes! No!" An alternative is "Do what you want!" or "I don't care!"

The silent treatment is punitive. Silences—as well as brief, terse, noncommittal responses—are weapons. We use them as a form of punishment when it seems our words as weapons have failed. Our silence, however, says a lot: If I can't best you with words, I'll get you with silence!

Silence is hard to deal with because it has the appearance of innocence. If we are asked about our silence we can even feign a surprise. "Is something wrong?" the other asks. "Something wrong?" we echo. "Who said anything was wrong?"

Of course nobody said anything was wrong—with words—but our nonverbal communication is saying loud and clear that something is indeed wrong. However, because it was not put to words we can act as though we were being abused by the very question.

Silence, we obviously believe, is safe. For some reason we assume that we are not accountable for the nonverbal communication of our silent treatment. So, in effect, becoming silent is a way of safely—we think— or protectively becoming a false witness. As Søren Kierkegaard said, "The safe thing to do is to be silent, for you will rarely be judged for what you don't say." But he goes on to say that keeping silent is the most dangerous way of all because one then risks losing something more important than being judged—namely, oneself. "What if by not venturing at all in the highest sense . . . I cowardly gain all earthly advantages—and lose myself?" (Kierkegaard, *The Sickness Unto Death*, ed. and tr. by H. V. Hong and E. H. Hong, pp. 34–35; Princeton, N.J.: Princeton University Press, 1980).

In attempting to escape the judgment that our communication is asking for, we are safe, but only from one danger. The other danger to which we are opened wide by our silence is that in escaping the judgment on our speech we are forfeiting the opportunity to grow through the encounter. For Kierkegaard such personal growth comes only from accepting the risk of putting the nonverbal communication into words.

Dwelling on Anger

Though silent, the silence of the silent treatment is an angry silence; the anger not only continues but may escalate. The emotional dimensions of this anger take over our minds and govern the way we reason.

Should it continue, we can become paranoid in our thinking.

"Paranoid" comes from the Greek words *para* and *nous*, which mean "beyond the reason." In this wild flight of mind we make irrational assumptions about the other and then build a rational assessment of the situation on this irrational base until our heightened imagination has led us in thought and ideas out of all proportion to reality.

Such anger goes contrary to the "rhythm of nature," James says. There is no listening to the feelings of the other, no empathy. The only feelings we identify with are our own in their supercharged intensity.

So there is wisdom inherent in James's bridle for the tongue that we be "slow to anger." For anger, though natural and belonging also to the divine, is a precarious passion for us human beings. But "slow to anger" does not mean "never be angry."

6

Denying vs. Affirming

The Bible has much to say about the passion of anger. It is not our purpose to present a complete study of this passion in the scripture, but rather to present a summation of this study. Happily, this is already done for us in the Bible itself. The Letter to the Ephesians does it in five words: "Be angry but do not sin" (Eph. 4:26).

Translation Difficulties

"Be angry but do not sin" is a hard saying and does not fit well with the mores of our culture—or perhaps other cultures as well. The imperative "Be angry" is the difficult part. In our plethora of modern translations it is frequently translated as a conditional clause, "If you become angry" (*Good News Bible* and *Anchor Bible* are examples). Since the Greek word is an imperative, giving an order, why the need to change to an "if" clause?

When the verse is translated as a conditional clause, "If you become angry," it puts the emphasis of the sentence on what follows: "do not sin." The reader's role is minimized in the conditional clause. "If you become angry" implies something that can happen *to*

one. On the other hand, *"Be* angry" emphasizes the
reader's own involvement in what happens. Beginning
with a conditional clause thus sacrifices the two em-
phases on involvement in the original wording, each
being equalized by the connecting conjunction. *Be*
angry but do *not* sin.

The Ephesian writer is actually quoting from Psalm
4:4: "Be angry, but sin not." Here again the translators
have their difficulties. But they are more justified in
this instance, since the Hebrew word translated "be
angry" (RSV) is literally "tremble." Some translate it
"tremble" (*Jerusalem Bible* and *New American Stan-
dard Bible*) and some translate it "tremble with fear"
(*Good News Bible*). *The New English Bible* uses the
equivalent of the conditional clause, "However angry
your hearts," even as it uses the conditional "if" in the
Ephesian verse.

"Trembling" suggests the physical manifestations of
either rage or terror. Yet, as we have seen, our rage
is often a secondary reaction to the more primary
passion of fear. So the distinction may not be all that
important.

The Septuagint version of the Old Testament, a
Greek translation of the third century B.C., translated
"tremble" as "be angry." It is from this version that
the Ephesian writer in all probability quoted, although
knowing the Hebrew original as well. Professor William R. Taylor, in his exegesis in *The Interpreter's
Bible,* concludes that "tremble" would literally be
understood as "be perturbed" or "be enraged" (vol. 4,
p. 32; Nashville: Abingdon Press, 1955).

It is understandable that there might be resistance
to using the imperative "be angry" if there were any
legitimate alternatives. When anger is viewed not
only as a precarious passion but also as a *negative*

passion, then one can readily perceive the conflict that hits the mind with a biblical imperative to *be* angry.

Affirming Our Anger

There is profound wisdom regarding this precarious passion in the most obvious translation, "Be angry, but sin not." But is it any wonder that most cultures, including ours, find it difficult to recognize? The wisdom in the verse is contingent upon accepting the imperative of being angry. Then one can understand how to control anger.

"Be angry" means *affirm* your anger. When anger is present in your emotional system, recognize it, accept it, own it. Do it by telling yourself and telling God, "I'm angry." Get it out into the open in your perception of the moment.

When you can recognize, affirm, and own your anger, you are in a good position to control it. In fact, without such awareness and acceptance, you will be at a decided disadvantage in directing your anger. Instead, it will direct *you*. In short, without the "be angry" in the first part of this two-part sentence, it is unlikely that we can carry out the second part, "sin not." The *not* depends on the *be*.

The tendency is to do the opposite—to deny rather than to affirm our anger. In fact, for many of us, denial or repression is our instinctive—that is, our unconsciously directed—reaction to the emergence of anger within us. You know the person who knows all the nonverbal as well as verbal signs of anger and yet, when somebody asks, "Why are you getting so angry?" replies, "Who's angry?" The implication is "I'm not!" Yet this person's anger is felt by all in the vicinity.

He or she may offer an explanation, however. "I'm

not angry, I'm just concerned [or upset, or annoyed]."
It seems we can only acknowledge our anger when
we designate it by one of these more acceptable
euphemisms.

Actually, I am describing myself. Everybody around
me knows when I am angry—but me. I tend to ra-
tionalize my anger behind euphemisms. Obviously I
do not want to think of myself as angry. Why not?

Even though we deny our anger, those persons in
our midst who are sensitive pick it up. Phil had always
thought of himself as an easygoing, even-tempered
man. His wife had given him many reasons to be
angry, but Phil seemed never to be bothered. But in
counseling with him and his wife I said something that
tripped his anger. Phil shot something back at me
which I have forgotten, but I have not forgotten his
eyes. They were blazing in my direction.

"You're angry," I said.

"Yes," he said, "I guess I am."

"I feel it," I said, "and it is directed toward me."

"No," Phil said, almost mechanically, "I'm not angry
at you, it's the situation I'm in—it bugs me."

As we continued to talk about his situation, it was
evident that Phil's inner self was in turmoil. Embar-
rassed by his wife's insensitivity over the years, he
had handled it by distracting himself in his work. But
six months previously Phil's plant had closed and he
had lost his job. In his state of unemployment he had
little opportunity, or motivation, to distract himself,
and his anger came out in ways that frightened him.
It was upsetting the image of himself with which he
felt comfortable. His anger had been percolating at
the periphery of his awareness for a long time and
now it had shifted toward the center.

It is hard to acknowledge our anger face to face with

the one with whom we are angry. We may be able to look back and see our anger, or describe it later to someone else. But to say "I'm angry with you" seems the most difficult of all, except, of course, when it gets beyond us and we "lose our temper."

Arthur Miller's character Quentin, in his play, *After the Fall,* embodies this inability of some of us to face our own anger—particularly when this anger is directed toward one with whom we are not supposed to be angry. Quentin could not tolerate his resentment toward his mother. She had educated him well on how much she had done for him and how much she expected from him. He was the star she saw rising to replace the fallen one who was now a failure in her eyes—his father. He should have been grateful to her, but instead he was angry.

The clue to the presence of this anger came in his response to his mother's death. He could not grieve. It was not just that he could not cry, for this could be due to shock. Rather, he was aware that *inwardly* he was not grieving her death. "I don't seem to know how to grieve" (Arthur Miller, *After the Fall,* p. 6; New York: Penguin Books, 1980).

Later he realized why. It's hard not to hate someone who asks so much of you. He acknowledged it fully: "I'm full of hatred" (ibid., p. 107). He had projected this hatred onto others—especially his wife. As Quentin finally realizes what is wrong with him, he offers this challenge: "Do the hardest thing of all . . . see your own hatred and live" (ibid., p. 108).

It is difficult to acknowledge anger—to be angry—when that anger is directed toward a family member we are obligated to love. It is difficult to live with such anger. So the hardest thing of all—see your own hatred and *live.*

Destructiveness of Repression

Repressed anger is not only hard on our minds, it is also hard on our bodies. As a source of inner tension and stress, repressed anger contributes to many physical illnesses. Denied natural expression, the energy of this passion becomes a debilitating influence on our health.

Repressed anger also shows itself in emotional distancing within the family. It forms a barrier between people as formidable as a physical barricade. When our anger lies sullen within us, we go through the motions of relating but without the emotional warmth associated with these motions. Actually, we don't *want* to be close to the other because we are too angry to do so. But usually we don't realize what the problem is.

Our hidden anger also gets in the way of our wholehearted involvement in family activities. We lack the enthusiasm, the positive passion, that allows these activities to be spontaneous and moving experiences. Our anger comes out in our passive resistance to cooperation—even for pleasure—except on a surface level.

With some people the anger comes out indirectly, seeping out sideways. These people meet life with an almost constant smile—sometimes even with a chuckle of laughter after anything they say. But while communicating amidst the smiles and chuckles, a dig slips out here and there. The receiver, however, has a delayed reaction to the dig. How can any cutting remark come through all those smiles?

About ten minutes later, however, one realizes one has been hit. It is as though the attacker had anesthetized the spot with smiles before plunging in the dagger. Yet the attacker may not even be aware that he or she has hit the other. Such persons may have so much anger concealed within them that it simply slips out whenever they open their mouths.

Is It Wrong to Be Angry?

People who deny being angry, when they obviously *are*, evidently believe it is *wrong* to be angry. They would rearrange those six words of the biblical directive from "be angry but do not sin" to "do not sin by being angry."

When I have talked with these people about this impression of their anger, they will frequently say that they received it from their Christian homes. Yet this impression is biblically untenable. How then does this happen?

Because we know that anger can lead to violence and that violence is wrong, we take the next step and reason that *anger* is wrong. So it is important to suppress anger as a way of controlling it.

But suppression leads to a very tenuous control. As we have seen, the anger breaks or slips out in one destructive way or another. Actually the fear needs to be reversed. It is repressed anger that can lead to violence.

At best, repressed anger saps our vitality. Anger is a passion. If we cannot tolerate a normal expression of this passion, it seems we cannot then be vital in any other way as well.

The image of the good Christian as one who has little if any anger and resentment settles particularly on the good Christian *woman*. She is long-suffering to the point of denying not only her anger but also her own needs. This may be one factor in the large amount of depression that particularly afflicts women in our culture. When our aggressive tendencies are

denied and throttled in order to live up to the image
of a good Christian woman, this repression of anger
may end up depressing the spirit.

Thus we see the wisdom of the biblical directive to
be angry but still not sin. By separating anger from
sin, the directive frees us to direct our anger into
constructive channels of expression. By affirming our
anger we legitimize it in human experience. So *be*
angry—but do not sin.

And Sin Not

In its biblical context, "do not sin" means do not let
your anger lead you into an arrogant judging of others.
In being critical of another's behavior—a child, perhaps, or a spouse—we do not attack the other's *person*.
Hurling judgments at the other's person can undermine his or her sense of self-worth. It is one thing to
say, "I am unhappy over the way you did that job"; it
is entirely another to say, "You never can do anything
right!"

When we hear such negative judgments on our
personal worth, we may begin to believe them. This
internalization of others' accusations takes its toll on
our self-image.

"Do not sin" means do not attack your own person
either—by depressing yourself over your failures. The
object of our anger is as often our own self as others.
The same self that we can depress we can also be
angry with.

Like our anger toward others, this anger toward
ourselves also needs a healthy outlet. I have found it
helpful on occasion to use words to tell myself that I
am angry with myself and why. It seems to do wonders
for lifting an incipient depressed mood over negative
experiences or behaviors.

"Do not sin" definitely means no physical violence. The many incidents of physical abuse of children, spouses, and older parents emerges out of our human inability to deal constructively with our anger.

Anger toward others or toward ourselves is a legitimate human reaction. So *be* angry. But find healthy ways to express or deal with it so that you do not let your anger lead you into sinning—against others or against yourself, and thereby also sinning against God.

When Silence Is Golden

In spite of its being a put-down on human speech, the aphorism "Silence is golden" grows out of human experience. There is a time when silence *is* golden—when, in our anger, to say nothing is the better course.

These are the times when we recognize our pattern of behavior and know from experience that our anger may well be a distorted reaction to our faulty perception. It is wise then to wait before verbally expressing our anger. If our awareness is correct, the anger is based more on "old-tape" projections than on present realities.

This is the wisdom behind the common advice to count to ten before you talk. It probably would be better in some instances to count to ten thousand. It is also the wisdom behind finding substitutional activities for draining our anger—like throwing ourselves into our work, or giving ourselves a physical workout, or trying to pull up a tree by the roots. In these alternate outlets we still need to acknowledge our anger to ourselves and to God. At the same time we are questioning whether we are not *over*-reacting and therefore need time or other safer outlets to help us sort things out.

We may then wisely restrain our tongues, believing

that our anger will dissipate as we regain a more objective perspective. We believe this because of our experience in living with and knowing ourselves. If we figuratively step aside in spite of our anger and observe ourselves in our reactions, we will exert a stabilizing influence on our imagination.

Our overreactions are comparable to a temporary paranoia. Our emotions are stimulated out of all proportion to what is supposedly the stimulus. We are reading too much into the situation—allowing old tapes to take over rather than letting the moment have its own identity. Suspicious eyes see suspicious behavior.

In our suspicious perspective we generate too much anger. If we resort to words at this time, they tend to come out too heavily for the circumstances. This further complicates the matter by creating additional obstacles to resolving it.

Choosing to remain quiet with our anger under these conditions is not repression, since the decision is made consciously and freely and not compulsively or subconsciously. Rather than being motivated by fear which characterizes a repressive decision, this decision is motivated by the wisdom of experience— from knowing ourselves and how we function.

Later we may be grateful—when our reasoning processes have been restored—that we did not say anything. We are relieved that we did not generate any strife over the situation since we no longer feel the way we did. At least there are no wounds to bandage or bad tastes to counteract.

It may be helpful then to share with the family where we were—but no longer are. Verbalizing what has transpired within us, in an atmosphere of trust, helps us in our commitment to act wisely rather than impulsively in our anger. It also may help others to understand us better in our vulnerability, and therefore to relate to us more intelligently and sensitively.

If you are in doubt about whether your anger is justified—at least in its intensity—it is wise to wait awhile before you speak. If the anger passes, then you have done nothing to make matters worse. On the other hand, if it remains—or even intensifies—you obviously need to take the steps necessary to deal with it.

But there is a warning in following these directives. How well do you know yourself? What are your tendencies regarding anger? If you generate anger quickly and blurt it out, the waiting period is the wiser course for you. But if you tend to hold back rather than speak, and your anger then dissipates—not because you realize you interpreted the incident faultily but because you are so used to stuffing it that it quickly vanishes on its own—you had best use words on the spot.

7

Healthy Ways of Expression

From our understanding of the biblical directive, "Be angry but sin not," we see that when we can affirm our anger we can also direct it. Clinical data from psychotherapy tell us virtually the same thing.

Taking It Out on Things

Some people choose to take their anger out on things. They not only acknowledge their anger, they also know they tend to overreact—and that their anger tends to be overly intense. Things are inanimate—they do not register pain.

The former manager of the Detroit Tigers baseball team, Fred Hutchinson, is an example of someone who chose to take his anger out on things. He had a volatile temper, with a tendency to verbal violence, and could cut his players down with his tongue.

Being a decent person, Hutchinson regretted these occasions. Being a practical person he also knew that verbal attacks could undermine a player's confidence so that he was less able to play well because of the verbal barrage.

So Hutchinson worked out a plan based on his knowledge of himself and how he functioned. When he was particularly irked by his players' performance during a game, he gave a hand signal as the game ended that indicated he wanted the players to stay out of the clubhouse until he invited them in. Alone in the clubhouse, Hutchinson let his anger out by kicking tables and throwing chairs until he was physically exhausted. Then he called in the players.

Hutchinson had discovered that after venting his anger in this way, his normal sensitivity and reason returned and he was able to say what he wanted to say to his players without attacking them personally. Rather than undermining their confidence, he was able to encourage it by giving them pointers for improvement.

Is it not childish to throw chairs and kick tables? Not if we mean childish as immature. Perhaps a better word is childlike. Think of a child selecting a toy as an object for his or her frustration. Instead of bashing baby brother or sister, the child bashes the toy instead. While toys can be expensive, they do not have feelings. They are good displacements for anger directed toward people.

Letting It Out to God

There are other ways—verbal ways—that are perhaps more adult than bashing *things*. Biblical personages, for example, particularly the psalmists, verbally expressed their anger to *God*. Their language is at times too violent for use in our churches. Visitors to our services may wonder what kind of group they are getting into when they hear this violent language.

Psalm 69, especially verses 19–28, is a good illustration.

> Thou knowest my reproach,
>> and my shame and my dishonor;
>> my foes are all known to thee.

Insults have broken my heart,
   so that I am in despair.
I looked for pity, but there was none;
   and for comforters, but I found none.
They gave me poison for food,
   and for my thirst they gave me vinegar to drink.

Let their own table before them become a snare;
   let their sacrificial feasts be a trap.
Let their eyes be darkened, so that they cannot see;
   and make their loins tremble continually.
Pour out thy indignation upon them,
   and let thy burning anger overtake them.
May their camp be a desolation,
   let no one dwell in their tents.
For they persecute him whom thou hast smitten,
   and him whom thou hast wounded, they afflict still
      more.
Add to them punishment upon punishment;
   may they have no acquittal from thee.
Let them be blotted out of the book of the living;
   let them not be enrolled among the righteous.

A Catholic lay brother told me that his order uses these psalms along with the others in their daily worship. "We are a family," he said. "The family setting can absorb this kind of talk. It helps us to tune into our own emotional reactions to living so intimately with each other." In accepting the violent language of the psalms, the brothers could better accept their own corresponding violent feelings.

Job also is good with violent language. His verbal onslaughts are directed mostly against God. The most vividly violent of such expressions is in chapter 16:6–17.

If I speak, my pain is not assuaged,
   and if I forbear, how much of it leaves me?
Surely now God has worn me out;
   he has made desolate all my company.

And he has shriveled me up,
  which is a witness against me;
and my leanness has risen up against me,
  it testifies to my face.
He has torn me in his wrath, and hated me;
  he has gnashed his teeth at me;
  my adversary sharpens his eyes against me.
Men have gaped at me with their mouth,
  they have struck me insolently upon the cheek,
  they mass themselves together against me.
God gives me up to the ungodly,
  and casts me into the hands of the wicked.
I was at ease, and he broke me asunder;
  he seized me by the neck and dashed me to pieces;
he set me up as his target,
  his archers surround me.
He slashes open my kidneys, and does not spare;
  he pours out my gall on the ground.
He breaks me with breach upon breach;
  he runs upon me like a warrior.
I have sewed sackcloth upon my skin,
  and have laid my strength in the dust.
My face is red with weeping,
  and on my eyelids is deep darkness;
although there is no violence in my hands,
  and my prayer is pure.

In 19:7 Job even uses the word "violence" to describe how he feels. "Behold, I cry out, 'Violence!' but I am not answered; I call aloud, but there is no justice." God is not only abusing him, but also disregarding his pleas for an audience.

Job's words are strikingly similar to those used by the prophet Jeremiah under similar duress. "O LORD, thou hast deceived me, and I was deceived; thou art stronger than I, and thou hast prevailed. . . . For whenever I speak, I cry out, I shout, 'Violence and destruction!'" (20:7–8).

The word translated "deceive" can also be translated

"seduced." Jeremiah comes close to accusing God of raping him.

The fact that Jeremiah not only cries out the word "violence" but also shouts it shows the kind of emotional release that is taking place. Violence, rape, destruction, no justice—all are words of protest against what is happening. Whether it is the psalmist, Job, or Jeremiah, the charge is that this is an unfair world with an unfair God ruling over it, and I am the victim of this unjust conspiracy.

It is evident that these blasts of verbal violence are therapeutic. The key to the therapy is not only this violent letting go of feelings, but also letting go in the consciousness of God's presence. It is an exercise in cathartic prayer, which actually reduces the possibility of acting out the hostility toward others or themselves.

In contrast to us human beings, God has no fragile ego. God can take the barrage. We are not informing God of anything God does not know when we put words to our violent feelings. Rather, we are using words in all their intensity to help us resolve our emotional conflicts. We are exercising our God-given freedom to be in charge of our anger in our relationships with others, especially in the family. Letting it out to God prepares us for expressing our anger to others in ways that are constructive.

Speaking the Truth in Love

The Ephesian letter provides a parallel directive to "Be angry but do not sin," to guide us in this expression of our anger to others; it is "speaking the truth in love" (4:15). We are to use our tongue to tell the truth about ourselves to others, but also to do so in a loving way. Both speaking the truth and speaking it in love are equally important. We can speak the truth in an unloving way and do harm with the truth. Also we can speak falsehood in a loving way and do harm by our good intentions.

Speaking the truth in love is described in our day as an "I message." I as subject tell another the truth about myself as object. As an example, wife to husband: "I feel badly about what happened between us last night."

The I message is in contrast to a "you message," in which we make the other the subject and ourselves the object. As an example: "You hurt me by what you said last night."

When we use you messages in expressing our anger we are likely to tell the other off. The "you" will be followed by a verb that accuses.

The feelings we express in both an I and a you message may be similar, but the form in which they are expressed is different. This in turn can make a difference in their effect on the other.

This difference has its origin in our purpose for choosing the form. The purpose for the I message is to tell it like it is; the purpose for the you message is to accuse the other. In the I messages we describe the effects of the other's behavior on us. In the you message we attack the person of the other. As an example: "I am feeling thoroughly rejected in our relationship," versus, "You are a cruel, mean s.o.b.!"

Our purpose in speaking the truth in love is not to punish, to hit back, to retaliate, to make the other hurt for the hurt that he or she has inflicted on us. Rather, the purpose is to resolve the anger and salvage the relationship.

The effect on the other is likely to differ according to the purpose of our speaking. The you message usually brings an instinctive defensiveness that quickly becomes a counteroffense. The I message is more likely to bring concern, even curiosity. For example, imagine yourself being approached with the I message "I don't feel good about what happened last night. Would you not be inclined to ask why or to acknowledge that you do not feel good about it either? In so responding you open a dialogue rather than start an argument. You want to draw the other out for more clarity about his or her feelings.

Stimulus-Response Relationships

Family relationships are stimulus-response relationships. Living close together makes it likely that family members will be continually interacting with each other. Since these interactions can become habit patterns in relating, we become dependent upon the other to repeat the patterns.

We may interact differently with another when the two of us are alone. Siblings may behave differently toward each other when a parent is present. They may even interact differently depending upon which parent is present. Spouses may interact differently—at least on the surface—when the children are present.

Eric Berne has classified these interactions as specific kinds of "games," and the total interaction patterns as scripts. They have become games because they are so habitually predictable that they bypass any relating in depth, and also because it takes at least two to play them. The overall pattern of verbal interchange is like a script because the specific games we play are part of a larger pattern of interchange that is as predictable in its interactions as though it were a script we had memorized.

If, however, one family member changes—that is,

does something other than follow the predictable stimulus response-patterns—the other members are confronted with a new situation. The stimulus is different, and therefore the response also should be different. But it may not be—at least at first. The hope is that with the repetition of the stimulus the other finally will come forth with the appropriate response.

This interdependency of stimulus and response in family relationships provides a counselor with a way to help a troubled marriage or parent-child relationship when only one of the family members comes for counseling. The counselor can assist the person who comes to improve the stimuli that he or she is putting into the relationship. The counselor can also assist the person to change his or her responses to the other's stimuli when those responses perpetuate a destructive exchange.

As the counselee is able to effect these changes in his or her stimuli and responses in the relationship, the other in the relationship is confronted with a new kind of stimulus and an unexpected kind of response.

Since we are creatures of habit, the new stimuli from the counselee may not bring a different response at first from the other. But they will create a problem for the other. His or her behavior is hardly justified by this new way of interacting. Things no longer fit. The unfamiliar can throw us for a loss. The other may even resent the counselee's not playing the game or following the script. But persistence on the counselee's part may ultimately effect change also in the other. Through the counseling, the counselee has learned to use the soft answer that turns away wrath in place of the harsh word that stirs up anger (Prov. 15:1).

But there are times when the soft answer is the problem. The passive counselee may need to learn to

take a more self-affirming position in family relationships. Instead of caving in to pressure, the counselee
may learn how to remain firm.

In no longer playing the role of the passive adapter
in the game, the counselee may realize that the game
was also a protection for him or her. When we take
the passive role it is usually because we fear the
imagined consequences of being assertive. Before we
can change our response, we who play the passive role
may first have to deal with our fear. Since we never
know for sure how another will respond to our unanticipated assertive stance, we obviously have some
justification for our fear.

Children also can learn to express their feelings in
a healthy way. The modeling of such expression in
their parents, of course, is the most effective way of
teaching. But children can be taught the use of the I
message, just as they can be taught other behavior
patterns. Instead of laying it on their parents with a
you message, "You always let him have *his* way," the
child can learn to express this sibling conflict by using
an I message, "I'm feeling that I don't count around
here." Instead of "You're always on my back," the
child could learn to say, "I feel like I'm not being
trusted."

The I message is closer to the truth than the you
message, because it does not lay the responsibility for
how we feel on another. It is truthful because it tells
what is going on within us. It is loving because its
purpose is to repair a relationship rather than attack.
As a congruent use of language, an I message gives
the other the needed knowledge for intelligent relating.

Our children were fortunate to begin their education
with a first-grade teacher who used language in this
congruent way. As she described her approach to us
in a PTA meeting and as our children confirmed it to

us, she made it a point to let the children know where
she was emotionally. Most of us have our emotional
ups and downs, and she was no exception. When she
arrived at school in a flat or even irritable mood, she
told the children rather than attempting to hide her
feelings.

"Children," she would say. "Miss Cargill is in a bad
mood today, so please be careful. I don't want to be
cross with any of you, but I may if you are not careful."
The children knew where she was.

But suppose she had attempted to conceal her negative feelings behind a forced smile. The first child
who stepped out of line would have received the load
of her negative feelings. His impression then would
be, She sure doesn't like *me*!

But suppose even after warning the children, it
happened anyway. What then is the child's response?
"She's right—she sure *is* in a bad mood!" The difference between these two responses tells the difference
in the effect of the reprimand on the child.

The I message form of speaking the truth in love is
not likely to be a manipulative tactic since in its sentence structure, at least, it does not invade the other's
space. If the speaker's person is in harmony with this
structure, he or she is seeking to dialogue with the
other rather than to control or to possess the other.

But of course the person may not be in harmony
with this structure of speech. One may still seek to
control the other under the guise of speaking the truth
in love.

If a person is manipulatory, however, the use of the
I message will be distorted by the attitude of the
speaker. Even though the words are correctly spoken,
the attitude of the speaker will communicate louder
than the chosen words. The hidden agenda behind
the I message will have more effect on the relationship

than the I message itself. Even if the words are appropriately chosen for speaking the truth in love, they will be heard as inappropriate.

The purpose of a structure of speech such as an I message is to provide our already present attitude—namely, love—with the wisdom needed to communicate effectively. If you desire a better relationship for its own sake with your spouse, child, parent, in-law, the I message will provide you with the opportunity to express your conflicts, including your angry feelings, in a congruent and caring way.

8

How It Works

As we have noted previously, anger is often a secondary emotion in family conflicts. It is the reacting emotion to one's feelings of fear, or guilt, or hurt. If we allow our anger to lead us to the more primary passions to which it is a reaction, we will get down to business sooner on what is troubling us in our relationship. Then, if we can express this *primary* passion, we will be communicating where we need to communicate.

Seeing What Is Behind Our Anger

After feeling, and perhaps also expressing, our anger toward someone in the family who has interrupted what we were trying to say in order to talk about something else, we may realize that behind our anger at this apparent rudeness is the hurt we feel in being cut off.

If we are aware of our hurt we also can express it. "When you interrupt me when I am trying to say something, I feel hurt." Now the other must deal with the consequences of his behavior: "I didn't mean to hurt you—it's just that you were going on and on." "It may have seemed that way to you," we say, "but I wasn't finished and I don't appreciate being stopped."

Or suppose after doing your best to complete a family chore, you are met with criticism rather than praise. This hurts—but it also makes you mad. Again after realizing or expressing your anger, you may also be aware of your hurt feelings. Now is the opportunity to go to the heart of the matter.

"When you criticized the way I did the job I felt hurt. I put a lot of time and effort into that job, and it hurts when it seems not to be appreciated." Now the other has to deal with the consequences of his or her critical approach, which an angry exchange alone would only prevent.

I have found this insight into the more primary emotion very helpful in my own family relationships. On one memorable occasion it provided the needed breakthrough in what seemed to be an insoluble conflict with my teenage son.

The setting is one that every parent of teenagers can empathize with and every teenager can commiserate with: learning to drive the family car.

Five times already, I had been through the harrowing experience of sitting beside a new driver as he or she fulfilled the required practice hours. Now I was challenged by the last child. You would think I would be quite proficient in driver education by this time, but actually I was getting worse. I am by profession a teacher, but when it comes to teaching a family member to drive the car, I am a deteriorated teacher.

The incident to which I refer occurred after church on a particular Sunday. This is probably the most hazardous time for families, since, in having been to worship together, one supposes nothing bad can happen between them. This illusion sets us up for a fall.

My new driver said, "Can I drive home from church?" My wife headed for the back seat. My reason overcame my feelings as I said, "Might as well."

So I seated myself tensely beside the driver. As we were driving along, I noticed bicyclers ahead of us. "Slow down," I said. Nothing happened. I repeated it—"I said slow down"—this time with increased volume.

"I did," my son answered.

"You did not," I said. "I've been watching your feet—you didn't put your foot on the brake."

"No," he said, "I took my foot off the accelerator."

"Listen," I said. "When I say slow down, I mean, Put your foot on the brake!"

"My driving instructor says when you are in a line of traffic you slow down by taking your foot off the accelerator."

This pushed my button. I see red when a driving instructor who assigns the parent to do all the work is used as an authority against me. Every parent knows my next line.

"When I'm sitting beside you *I* am your driving instructor!"

"Then you'll just confuse me and I'll flunk my driving test!" he shouted.

"Then flunk it," I yelled. Talk about a script!

After that it was sullen silence. Anyone gifted with extrasensory perception would have perceived heat waves coming up through the top of the car. As we arrived home my son got out of the car as fast as he could and slammed the car door. Even as I met sullen silence with sullen silence, so I met slamming doors with slamming doors. I can slam a door as hard as you can, I said to myself. And I did.

But when I got into the house, all my intensity drained from me. "What's wrong with me, God?" I asked. "Why am I getting worse and worse at this business?"

When you ask God for enlightenment, you might

just get it. At least I did. At that moment I saw clearly why I was so worked up. I was scared! My anger was my reaction to my fear. Or was it panic?

Should I tell my son? Do fathers tell their teenage boys that they are scared? They do when they have just had an answer to prayer. So I went to him.

"I think we need to talk," I said.

"What about?" he asked.

"What about?" I said. "About what happened on the way home from church. We don't want to have a fight every time you take the wheel."

"Oh, that," he said through tightened lips. "That's simple. It's your car—we'll do what you want." These kids know how to get us.

"No," I said. "That's not what I want. I want to tell you something I don't think you know."

"What's that?" he asked.

"Are you aware that I am frightened when I'm sitting there beside you?"

"Frightened?" he said. "What are you frightened of?" The naïveté was genuine. Why would I be frightened just because a teenage novice is in charge of a couple of tons of steel?

"It's not just you," I said. "You're simply the last of a long line. First there was your mother. I remember the time when we were turning the corner and I thought the oncoming car in the other lane was awfully close. But I assured myself that it was just because I was sitting next to the driver, where I was not used to sitting. And then, *Whambo!* We clip the car's fender.

"Then there was your sister. I remember thinking to myself, We're awfully close to the curb. But again I decided it was because I was not used to sitting so close to the curb. And then—up we went over the curb into someone's front lawn right after a heavy rain.

"Then there was your brother. We were coming

into the garage, and it seemed we were very close to the right side. Again I reminded myself that I was sitting where I was not used to sitting. Things obviously wouldn't look the same. And what do you know? We clipped the garage door and exchanged its white paint for our gray.

"So when I see bikes ahead, I remember all those other times, and I see you already hitting them. That's why I'm scared."

"I see," he said, obviously subdued. "Well, I'll try to remember that you're scared."

That deserved a quid pro quo. "If you do that," I said, "I'll try to remember that you have a driving instructor."

"Thanks," he said. "Thanks a lot!"

Well, we got through it. He did his best not to frighten me, and I did my best to remember that he had a driving instructor. It was a plan we both owned.

I hate to think of what might have happened in the practice days ahead of us, if I had not seen what was behind my anger and used an I message to tell my son.

False Sense of Protection

Too often when our primary passion is fear we tend to conceal it because of our desire to protect the other. This is particularly true of men. But usually men are also protecting themselves when they conceal their fear. They fear the possible tension that could occur if they revealed the truth about themselves. What would happen to the other's impression of us if we told them we were frightened?

There are times when we are probably right in concealing our fear out of concern for the other. If a child or spouse is already hanging on by the fingernails,

sharing our own fears may only add to theirs. It may
also deprive them of the support they need at the
moment to cope with their problems.

But too often we conceal our fears and also our guilts
and hurts as a way of coping with them. This shows
a lack of confidence in ourselves. Perhaps we should
deal directly with these primary feelings, even though
they are uncomfortable. We may be surprised at how
well we can cope with the truth—even about ourselves.

We also need to face the possibility that not sharing
our fears and hurts with family members shows a lack
of acceptance of these members in their ability to cope
with the truth about *us*. We may be assuming they
cannot rise to the occasion. This very assumption, or
lack of faith in them, may prevent them from doing
so.

While there is a legitimate need to protect family
members from having more than they can cope with,
we need also to raise the question about whether this
protective attitude is really necessary. Being a pro-
tector may give us a sense of importance in the relationship, but it also may prevent the relationship from
developing into a relationship of mutual respect. It
also may hinder rather than help the growth of the
one we seek to protect.

9

Putting Words to the Positive

Even positive feelings can go unexpressed in the family—probably more so than negative feelings. There is an amazing reluctance to put words to our positive feelings toward others, and this reluctance extends beyond the family into society as a whole.

Why Are We Reluctant?

As I left my place of work on one occasion I was thinking how fortunate we were to have such excellent secretarial help. These secretaries were not only competent but generous, cheerful, and helpful. The thought then struck me, Why are you telling yourself this? Go tell the secretaries!

My immediate reaction was negative. No need to do that. But since I could give no rational answer to why there was no need to do it, I forced myself to go back and tell them what I had been thinking. Obviously they felt good to hear it. Why then was I so reluctant to do it?

I have heard students say, regarding their parents, particularly their fathers, "My father has never told me that he is proud of me, but I have heard from others that he has told *them*." Why would a parent conceal his or her good feelings toward a child from the *child*?

I know of one father who confided to his spouse that he did not deem it wise to compliment his children because they might become conceited.

Even if we don't use the word "conceited," others of us may fear that our compliments will lead someone to become overconfident, or even careless, thinking that he or she has it made. In other words, if people know they have succeeded in achieving our good impression of them, they will no longer have this motivation to do well. So they will sluff off and become careless with their efforts.

The strategy behind our reluctance to speak the positive is to keep others guessing regarding how we feel about them. They will stay on their toes if they don't know how they stand.

Another reason for our reluctance may be that we take our positive feelings about others for granted. The rationale is that we are owed what we are receiving from the other.

This is a similar kind of thinking to that which moves us to focus on the negative rather than the positive. While we take the positive for granted, the negative outrages us. The rationale is that such things should not happen to us. So we tend to focus on what we *don't* have—our deprivations—rather than on what we *do* have—our blessings. The result is discontent, which moves us only to attempts to remove the negative, rather than gratitude, which moves us to enjoy what we have.

The Positive Is Not Pressing

Obviously, positive feelings are not as pressing as negative feelings. Joy, for example, is a pleasant sensation compared to anger, which is uncomfortable. Both are invigorating, but only one, anger, is aggravating.

Positive feelings, therefore, are *enjoyed* more than they are *shared*. But if we shared them, would we not spread the joy and enjoy them more?

Recall Sam, in chapter 3, the husband who found it difficult to put words to his positive feelings for Carol, his wife, and confined himself to nonverbal symbols of appreciation, such as coming home for lunch. Like Sam, we may withhold the support that others need from us because we find it difficult to say honestly how we feel toward them. The resistance seems to stem primarily from the fact that these feelings are *positive*.

For our own integrity as well as for others' self-confidence, we need to put words to these feelings. Doing so makes us congruent—the same on the outside as on the inside. Since few of us would not acknowledge that we like to hear good things about us, sharing our good feelings about others is a fulfilling of the Golden Rule. "As you wish that men would do to you, do so to them" (Luke 6:31). Putting words to our feelings then would be tantamount to saying, "Since I like feeling good about myself, I would like to help you feel good about *your*self."

Jesus was not reluctant to express positive feelings. Like the rest of us with whom he identified, Jesus probably felt the need for reassurance. He wanted to hear how his message was being received. So he sounded out his disciples (Matt. 16:13–17):

"Who do men say that the Son of man is?" They gave him what they had picked up—John the Baptist, Elijah, Jeremiah, or one of the prophets. Then Jesus put the question to them: "But who do you say that I am?" Immediately Peter answered, "You are the Christ, the Son of the living God." Obviously Jesus felt good to hear this. "Blessed are you, Simon Bar-Jona!" And this positive affirmation must also have made Peter feel good.

A Pathetic Bondage

But as indicated previously there are people who seem unable to speak directly to others about their good feelings toward them. Perhaps they never were the recipients of this good experience themselves, particularly in their developing years, and without models seem incapable of doing it.

Or perhaps they are subconsciously resisting: Nobody has praised *me* or helped me feel good about myself. Why should I do it for others? While not consciously said to oneself, this may be what is coming through. Or, to put it in family terms: If my father [mother] didn't do it for me, why should I do it for *my* children?

I've been with families where the parents may well have reasoned in this manner. At least they never seemed able to say anything good about their children *to* their children. As is frequently the case, however, they were quite free in saying critical things to their children.

There are siblings who, even as adults, when all their developmental rivalry should be over, still cannot tell their siblings anything positive. There are spouses who also seem to be in this same kind of bind; they cannot for the life of them put direct words to any tender, kind, or otherwise positive feelings that they have about the other.

Of course, one could argue that they probably don't have the good feelings to start with. Maybe so. But I'm inclined to think the obstacle is in putting words to these feelings, rather than in not having them. But as we shall see, putting words to them tends to encourage even the speaker to feel better.

This reluctance to speak the positive continues outside the family. Some pastors have a hard time saying positive things about their people. There are parishioners who seem unable to say these good things about their pastor, as though they were locked into an adversary role with this symbol bearer of divine authority. And employers may have this same reluctance to express positive appreciation to their employees.

This taboo on positive affirmation stifles both the growth of personal relationships and the growth of the persons themselves. Those who function under this taboo are in a pathetic bondage of the spirit. They have never seen the light in the eyes of others when these others receive affirmation. They have never had anybody say to them, "You've made my day!" In withholding the joy that their tongue could give, they are robbing themselves of the joy they could receive.

Those Who Depreciate the Gift

Some people, on the other hand, make it hard for those who want to reinforce them. They turn off the words and leave the giver feeling uncomfortable. They themselves, of course, are uncomfortable when anything positive is said about them, and so they are less than gracious to the speaker.

Perhaps you have had this happen to you. The person's response to your positive words left you confused. He or she looked away from you, gave no smile, mumbled something like, "I don't know about that," and became busy with something else—or quickly changed the subject.

You wonder, Did I say it badly? Does he or she think I was insincere—or trying to flatter? By this time you probably regret having said anything. Instead of feeling good for having shared your good feelings about the other, you feel the person has dismissed you. Perhaps you were wrong in your judgment, and the other wrote you off as a superficial observer?

As we can see, the giver needs reinforcement also. One takes a risk even in expressing *positive* feelings. The receiver's gracious reception provides this reinforcement, which in turn is an encouragement for the giver to give again.

So if you are a receiver, use words to express your appreciation to the giver: something like "I'm glad you feel that way" or "thanks for saying so."

Some of us find it difficult to be gracious receivers because we want to appear modest. If we accept the gift of somebody's good words we feel ill at ease. Our image of being modest is threatened, and so we protect ourselves by deprecating the words themselves.

We may still have received a surreptitious good feeling from the good words. Our deprecating words or actions, however, have successfully concealed it. But in so doing we have been insensitive to the needs of the giver.

In the workshops in spiritual growth that my wife and I facilitate, we have an exercise in which people list their strengths. Some have a difficult time with this. They would be more comfortable listing their weaknesses. They may even be unable to list any strengths.

In the sharing session that follows, others share with these people the strengths they perceive in them. Often they are met with qualifiers of some kind: "Yes, but you don't see me at other times," or "But the quality you mention is also my weakness." So we have devised a rule in the workshop. There is only one gracious response to the one who verbalizes your strengths to you: "Thank you."

When I asked Sam's wife, Carol (chapter 3), how it felt when Sam finally expressed his positive feelings with words, she said, "Good!" Sam needed to know this. It was an encouragement to do it again.

So the questions that all the Sams and Carols need to ask themselves are: What do I have against speaking the truth to the other, and especially speaking it in love? Why should I withhold the truth about my feelings if speaking it helps the other feel good? Also, if I feel good hearing good things about me, why not be honest and say so, particularly when doing so would support the other for saying these words?

All of us can give support to those in our families and beyond. It is unkind to withhold this support. It is like not giving food to the hungry. By the same token, we all can show appreciation to those who offer us support. It is unkind to withhold this appreciation, since the other needs it after taking the risk of putting words to positive feelings.

Reinforcement as Manipulation

Some have misused this gift of support to gain control over the other. This is always a temptation in gift giving. What do we want in exchange? If we want something, is it really a gift? If my gift of positive words is my way of getting you on my side in whatever it is I am attempting to do, it is simply a "nice" way of attempting to manipulate you.

The hidden agenda behind the gift is to get the desired response from the receiver. This is a way of trying to control the receiver. If I say nice things about you, you will like me, and I can use this goodwill as an investment for when I need it. Or if I say I like your work, and I have a stake in your work, you will work harder because of my reinforcement, and I will reap the benefit.

Employers can exploit their employees in this way. Also, teachers can exploit their pupils, clergy their parishioners, parents their children, and vice versa. We recognize this tendency by the familiar crass response to receiving positive words: "What do you want?" Evidently this manipulative agenda behind gift giving is so prevalent that we view the giver with suspicion.

I recall a student of mine who viewed my positive words about his test as manipulatory. So he flunked his next test deliberately as a way of saying, You thought that by praising my work you would get me to keep it up or even improve. This shows you that you can't control me like that.

Ironically, by deliberately failing his next test the student was giving me a control over him that I didn't want. He reasoned by rebelling, by doing the opposite of what he thought I wanted from him, that he was free from my influence. Actually, he was simply letting me influence him in a negative way. The rebel is as bound to the authority figure as the conformist. Neither is free to make decisions that are genuinely their own.

The Truth Comes Through

While the desire to manipulate through gift giving is always a possibility, the manipulators are ultimately revealed for who they are. Since the manipulator wants something in return, the spirit behind the words sooner or later will give itself away. Then we no longer take the words seriously. They have been shown to mean little in themselves. They have been cheapened to meet the needs of the giver.

I deal with letters of recommendation, which accompany student applications for admission to seminary. How seriously do we take these letters? Usually it depends on who is writing them. If the letter comes from someone who consistently writes letters of praise, we evaluate it lightly. The recommender has a need to be supportive that blinds his or her observation of the person. But if it comes from someone who has shown a capacity to speak forthrightly about both positive and negative observations, we value it highly. Although it hasn't happened yet, I suppose if I received a letter from someone whom I perceived as consistently overly critical, I would value the criticism lightly.

So the motive in putting words to our impressions is to tell the truth after we have allowed ourselves to perceive it. To communicate our appreciation of others when that appreciation is genuine is to be congruent. Our motive may also be to provide reinforcement when that reinforcement can be honestly given. Because we know from our own experience how much we need this reinforcement at times to hang in there, we want to give what we also need.

And in this instance, as in others, the giver also receives. He or she receives the pleasure that comes from receiving the other's appreciation. If we are rewarded by a deepening of the relationship because of our gift, we can accept it gracefully. It's a great exchange when both giver and receiver can say, "You've helped to make my day!"

10

The Block to Change

Minding our tongue so that we do not use it to sin against our loved ones takes more than learning new verbal patterns in which to express our negative feelings. We also need a picture of ourselves in our minds that enables us to break from old and destructive patterns so that we can adopt new and constructive ones.

Feeling Bad About Oneself

The term "psychological powerbase" has been coined to describe the potential of our feelings of positive regard for ourselves. Douglass Lewis incorporates it in his first principle of conflict management: "Help others feel better about themselves" (*Resolving Church Conflicts*, p. 49; San Francisco: Harper & Row, 1981).

It is only logical that we would feel badly about ourselves if we have verbally abused a loved one. If, as James indicates, the tongue is a symbol of evil because of what we humans do with it, then to experience guilt over this verbal abuse is the natural consequence. Our behavior registers on our conscience. We judge ourselves and subsequently get down on ourselves. If this down-on-ourselves attitude persists, we develop what we call in our culture a "low self-image."

The low self-image is an obstacle in the way of changing our verbal styles—of minding our tongue— in our family relationships. This is why feeling good about ourselves is so important to effect these changes. Lewis explains (p. 50):

> Who has not experienced the effect of feeling bad about him or herself? . . . Our perceptual frames begin to close in. We become more narrow in our vision, in what we can hear or perceive, and in what we are willing to accept about ourselves. At the same time, we have less energy to act . . . less confidence . . . less belief that we can achieve our chosen goals.

Freud observed what he termed a "repetition compulsion" in human behavior. We humans tend to repeat compulsively our behavior patterns when confronted by familiar stimuli in our relationships, particularly those behavior patterns over which we feel guilty. This repetition compulsion is nowhere more apparent than in the verbal patterns in families, particularly in family conflicts.

As we have noted, we use Berne's terms now to describe these repetition compulsions—old tapes, scripts, games. We even recognize our own tapes along with those of others. Frequently one stimulates the other into "playing the game." Here we go again, we say, caught once more in our stimulus response trap.

These tapes or patterns depend for their repetition on unresolved guilt, usually guilt over precisely these behavior patterns. As this guilt becomes a habitual state of mind, it takes on the characteristics of the low self-image. What results is a chronic state of distorted perception—of self, life, and others—that perpetuates destructive behavior patterns, chief among which are *verbal* patterns. This low self-image is what Lewis describes as "feeling bad about oneself."

A Form of Guilt

The low self-image is not usually considered a form of guilt. The term has become so commonly used that it might well be described as a cultural malady. Descriptively, a low self-image means that deep down, underneath our various ways of interacting in our relationships, we do not think much of ourselves. Even when we engage in bragging, we may continue within ourselves to have these personal misgivings. Some of us succeed in repressing this awareness, but this does not alter the effect of the low self-image on our behavior.

Though I referred to the low self-image as a malady of our culture, it is obviously not confined to our culture or our time. Job in the Old Testament, for example, expressed his state of mind in his ordeal in terms strikingly similar to those we associate with the low self-image. "Oh, that I had the indictment written by my adversary!" he cried (Job 31:35).

The adversary in the prologue of the Book of Job is Satan, but in the poetic section of the book from which this quotation is taken, Job's adversary is actually God. Job wanted the indictment spelled out by God because he was pressured by his three friends to feel guilty over the calamities that had befallen him. Yet he could recognize no actions, no justification to which to attach his guilt. He wanted clarity, a specific indictment. He was being convicted of not measuring up—but to what? Because the judgment he felt lacked objective justification, his guilt was not only nebulous but also unresolved. In this state of mind, God or the universe is not our advocate but our adversary.

There is a close similarity between the feelings associated with a low self-image and those feelings of guilt we experience when we have said something that hurt a loved one or failed to say something that would have given support. But with the low self-image there is no specific action or lack of action—no scale of values—to which to attach the feelings of guilt. Instead, there is simply an arbitrary and rigidly applied judgment, usually picked up from how we perceive we are received in our social setting.

The feelings associated with the low self-image are best understood as feelings of shame—not shame over having *done* something shameful but shame over being who we are.

Brenda was a single mother trying to rear three children in a setting over which she felt little control. Her children were subjected to a strong subculture of drugs and sexual promiscuity in the neighborhood and the school. Already stretched to her limits by her job responsibility and her parental responsibility and her homemaking responsibility, Brenda was stretched beyond her limits when things started to go wrong with her children.

When one child stayed out all night and another came home stoned, Brenda broke down. "I've had it with being a parent," she sobbed. "I'm no good at it— I want out!"

Brenda felt she was a loser as a mother. There were no specific acts of failure in parenting that stood out in her mind; rather, she felt everything about it was a failure.

Her low self-image as a parent was due in part to her children's problems, but it was also due to cultural pressures to gain acceptance by her achievement, her production, her success as a mother.

In her low self-image as a mother, Brenda felt guilty

just for being who she was. Her failure as a mother as determined by our culture's standards was equivalent to her failure as a person. Ironically, our culture does not put this pressure on the father. Rather, the pressure on the man is to produce in his *job*.

The competition that characterizes our culture extends also to families. Brenda felt she was a failure as a mother in comparison to other mothers. Her children were doing poorly compared to other children. How children "do" reflects on the parents'—particularly the mother's—worth in the community. Brenda's children were doing poorly at school and with drugs, so Brenda considered herself a failure.

This competition between families makes it hard to rejoice in other children's "successes." We smile and say, "Good for you," but inwardly wish it were our child who was doing so well.

Our attitude toward our children is colored by this competitive pressure to compare them with other children. Since our own self-image is tied up with this cultural pressure, it is understandable why parents can become part of the pressure on our children.

Guilt Before Whom?

We are born with the capacity for a conscience. Since a low self-image is guilt over our total person, the judgment is coming from this evaluator within us. While the capacity for conscience is inborn, its development depends on our relationships. The family is the basic influence in this development, including the development of the standards by which this conscience does its evaluating.

We frequently bring the influence on our conscience from our family of origin into the development of our present family life. When this influence from the past is distorted, it of course perpetuates distortion in the present. Jean's father, for example, exploited his influence over her developing conscience by using the guilt he could extort from it to control her. By conditioning her to believe that he was always right and that obedience to him was the same as obedience to God, he still had his hook into her when she was in midlife.

"He makes unreasonable demands on me," Jean said, "but I don't feel right inside until I give in. Yet I know in my head that I'm not really helping him or myself by doing this."

In her present family, Jean has continued to find her peace of conscience by giving in. She and her husband have had many disagreements, but sooner or later her husband knows that Jean will acknowledge that he was right. Her teenage children also notice this tendency in her disagreements with them. Peace of conscience comes to Jean only when, after having a legitimate disagreement, she acknowledges that she is the one who is wrong.

How can Jean become free—even in midlife—from these built-in guilt trips that are as predictable as clockwork? Certainly not from attacking guilt per se as though this uncomfortable passion were the culprit. The key to her freedom is in knowing who is really her God.

Obviously Jean's father is not her God. Yet she has invested him with the qualities of divinity by identifying his voice with the voice of God. At least she believes that her father and God stand together against her. Our mental picture of God, whether clearly envisioned or vaguely impressed, is always something less than God. In Jean's case it is considerably less.

It is hard not to get the impression in our developing years that we stand over against the adult world and that God is with that world. But the fact remains that God is other than a human authority figure. God alone is the Creator; the others are the created.

So also there may be a difference between guilt that stems from the confused picture of God in our minds and guilt before the One who is really God—a difference between guilt from a conscience based on this confusion and guilt stemming from our understanding of the Word of God.

Inherent in our maturation to adulthood is this need to differentiate between God and parents or other significant adults. This differentiation as it pertains to our conscience is expressed by Paul. "It is a very small thing that I should be judged by you or by any human court," he wrote to the Corinthians. "I do not even judge myself. . . . It is the Lord who judges me" (1 Cor. 4:3–4).

When our mental picture of God is distorted by human authority figures, our picture of ourself is also distorted. We internalize the judgments of these authority figures on us—or at least our impression of these judgments—thus making them our own judgment on ourself. Then we lack a center or focus within ourselves which is distinctly our own. The guilt we experience before our internalized judgment upon ourselves is no more reliable than is the judgment itself. But the only way it can be discounted is by recognizing who really is our God.

The Value of Guilt

In contrast to guilt as the nebulous discomfort associated with a low self-image, conscious and clearly defined guilt over specific behavior is a characteristic of a mature person. Guilt of this nature is based on an internalized moral, ethical, and spiritual value system with which we choose to identify. When we transgress or fail to live up to these values in our relationships, our sensitized conscience registers guilt. We *feel* it. We need this discomfort of guilt to bring our behavior into our reflective consciousness so that we can evaluate it according to standards we ourselves have espoused.

Guilt is the indicator of our need to question our behavior. It provides a feedback on ourselves. Consequently, guilt is the prelude to change.

This rationale of guilt, however, is seldom either observed or experienced. Instead, our cultural awareness of guilt is that of an uncomfortable weight within us that binds us with its unrelenting judgment to the old ways rather than liberating us for the new. So guilt is basically an unproductive and therefore useless pain. If it only bound us to the old, this would be reason enough to resent it. But guilt, through its discomfort, diminishes any pleasure that still might have accrued to the old.

So it is understandable to see a bumper sticker with the words, SCREW GUILT! These words clearly express our culture's problem with guilt. It is not only a useless emotion, it is even harmful. So away with it!

It is significant that guilt should be dismissed in crude sexual terms, since much of our resentment of guilt is toward our guilt over sex. It gets in the way of our accepting sex as pleasure.

"Screw" has become a verb with negative overtones. It is a sexual synonym for attack—for rape. How ironic, in a day of supposed sexual emancipation, that a word for sexual intercourse is interpreted as an attack. Before the disease of AIDS came to inhibit sexual behavior, only guilt was judged to have that role. So attack guilt—screw it!

Our attitude toward guilt has much to do with its
having seeped into its less differentiated form of low
self-image. Since we cannot cope with guilt when it
comes to us straight, we force it into its more diffuse
sense of judgment: namely, shame. Ironically, in ig-
noring guilt or in attacking it, we end up with a more
severe judgment on ourselves than if we were to accept
guilt as a judgment, primarily on our *behavior.*

In spite of our problems in coping with it, the
experience of guilt is basic to our humanity. It is the
initial step in effecting change in our behavior. Yet
before it can function as this initiator for change, guilt
needs to be resolved. When our guilt remains unresolved, it actually becomes an *obstacle* to change.

When we persistently feel bad about ourselves—
that is, have a low self-image—we are functioning in
a state of self-rejection. This self-rejecting state of mind
makes us incapable of coping positively with family
conflicts. Instead, it binds us to our old destructive
ways, over which we feel guilty. Even as feeling good
about ourselves is a psychological power base for
adopting new verbal patterns such as the I message,
so the low self-image—being down on ourselves—is
a form of psychological impotence that locks us into
old verbal patterns such as the you message.

It is precisely at this point that the Christian faith
offers help. While we have all manner of movements
and schools of thought for elevating self-esteem in our
day of low self-esteem, the "old, old story" has been
in the business for a long, long time. As Jesus said,
he came to bring liberation to the captives, including
those captive to the unresolved guilt of the low self-
image, so that they could be free to be creative in
their relationships (Luke 4:16–21).

The gospel is good news for us precisely because

it brings us reconciliation with who we are so that we can enter into new ways of doing things. For our specific concerns, this means entering into new ways of using our tongue.

11

Forgiveness:
The Change Agent

Tom and his father were having difficulty getting along, a not uncommon occurrence when you are seventeen. After a particularly heated exchange, Tom's mother took him aside and said, "Tom, your father has a heart condition. It is not good for him to get so worked up. Please try to get along with him." But Tom was in no mood for restraint.

"Talk to *him*," he said tersely. "He's the one who started it."

Two days later the high school principal called Tom out of class. Putting his arm around him, he said, "Your father has had a heart attack. I'm taking you to the hospital."

But they didn't get there in time. As Tom heard the bad news from his mother as she met him outside his father's room, anybody close to him would have heard him say under his breath, "I killed him."

Tom was inconsolable. Continually he relived in his mind the argument he had had with his father, and each time he tried to say the right words so that it would end differently. Under the weight of guilt Tom was punishing himself by depressing himself, making himself miserable for what he believed he had done. His conscience, besides judging him, was also flailing him.

Forgiveness and Not Self-punishment

Self-punishment does not really relieve guilt, and reliving the bad scene in order to make it come out right cannot alter the facts. But Tom felt he needed to continue to do both. Perhaps it was part of his healing. Ultimately Tom will realize that forgiveness is the only real and complete answer to his self-loathing. As his self-punishing gives way to the reality of God's forgiveness, Tom will be moved to forgive himself and begin his life anew.

Unlike Tom, most of us have another chance to do things differently in our families. We are not confined like him to a fantasy world for our wish fulfillment. We need to take advantage of the opportunities that are still ours because people are still alive. This means first of all that we express our guilt over our role in our family relationships to God and let God forgive us. Then we will be free to effect the changes we desire in our behavior—particularly our verbal behavior.

The good news of the Christian faith is that God became one of us in Jesus so that, through Jesus, God could reconcile to God all of us whose guilt had made us prisoners of our past. The cross of Jesus is the symbol of this reconciliation, for it is through Christ's cross that God's forgiveness is given. In that cross God bore the suffering of all humanity so that we might be accepted as we are. God's compassion for us in our addiction to our destructive ways has opened the way for our freedom.

Since it is God who wants to forgive us—to accept us as we are—can we let it happen? Can we let God's good news be our good news? When we allow God to love us just the way we are through the gift of forgiveness, it is possible to feel good about ourselves. The hold of the low self-image over us is broken.

How can you feel good about yourself? By knowing you are loved by God. The cross of Christ is the overwhelming assurance of this love, for it comes through the pain and suffering of the Giver. God not only feels our pain, it is also God's pain.

Even as being down on ourselves binds us to our past, so feeling good about ourselves frees us from our past to make changes in our present. Douglass Lewis describes the contrast:

> On the other hand when our psychological powerbase increases, when we regard ourselves more positively, our perceptual frames open up. We begin to see more options for ourselves. More alternatives are perceived and we have more energy to work on these alternatives. We also hear and are more open to other people's needs and goals and can more easily affirm their validity. (*Resolving Church Conflicts*, p. 50)

Being forgiven ourselves makes it possible also to forgive others. Tom, for example, did not even think about forgiving his father after he was dead. It was only Tom who needed forgiveness then. But before his father died, Tom felt entirely different about his father. He was angry with him. He felt his father was overly critical of him. It was then—before his father's heart attack—that Tom and his father could both have used some mutual forgiveness.

Forgiveness lifts our heavy weight of guilt so that we can put words to our uncomfortable feelings in a healthy way. It also frees us to put words to our positive feelings, since it is easier to speak positively about others when we feel positive about ourselves. Because we are reconciled with who we are through forgiveness, there is no need to conceal our negative feelings or attitude. The only need is to find the most constructive way to express them.

Anything that focuses on reconciliation seems particularly designed for family living, where reconciliation is constantly needed to maintain the continuity of relationships. Reconciliation begins with our relationship to ourselves and then extends to all others in the family system. By keeping the channels of communication open, forgiveness helps the family system to function well.

Intimate living not only brings joy and elation but also irritation and hurt. If these irritations and hurts are not dealt with in a healthy way, they may prevent us from having the positive experiences of joy and elation. Forgiveness is the means for preventing our irritation and hurt from taking the joy out of our relationships.

Yet at the same time we are irritated or hurting we may even resist forgiveness. Tom, for example, might have felt defiant after that last uproar with his father. "I'm too angry, too hurt, too turned off, too full of hate, to forgive," he might have said. Obviously Tom and his dad needed to talk out their feelings toward each other with I messages before the channels between them could open sufficiently to entertain forgiveness. This is the goal of "talking it out." If that goal had been reached, the relationship between Tom and his dad would have opened to positive experiences that otherwise were shut off.

Horrendous hurts occur in families. The members feel abused, whether physically or verbally, or by silence or emotional rejection. Only forgiveness can bridge the alienation created by these hurts. But forgiveness must never be used to enable us to take more abuse. Rather, it is a means for dealing with the abuse. Forgiveness is the way of breaking out of our repetition compulsions so that we can speak and act in different ways—ways that are constructive.

From the way I've described it, forgiveness may seem like a miracle because of what it can accomplish. As an act of God for God's people, this is precisely what forgiveness is—a miracle. It is at the center of the gospel that distinguishes the Christian faith.

Forgiveness for the Inexcusable

But forgiveness is often watered down in our contemporary society. We identify it with understanding: "To understand," we say, "is to forgive." Yet forgiveness is not the same as understanding or excusing. We are not forgiven because we did the best we could, however poorly. We need forgiveness because we did *not* do the best we could.

We are not forgiven because our bad behavior was predisposed by our poor background. Bad behavior stemming from a flawed environment would be understandable and excusable. In contrast, forgiveness is given to one who could have done differently regardless of background—and *did not.*

Again, because forgiveness is not based on any rationale that minimizes the offense, it partakes of the miraculous. It is a gift from God that is in no way deserved because of our limitations.

When the prophet Isaiah had a vision of the presence of God while he was in the temple, he was smitten with guilt. "Woe is me! For I am lost; for I am a man of unclean lips, and I dwell in the midst of a people of unclean lips; for my eyes have seen the King, the LORD of hosts!" (Isa. 6:5).

Isaiah's guilt over his unclean lips corresponds to the biblical emphasis on our use of the tongue as the key to who we are. In the vision in the temple Isaiah's lips were cleansed. An angel with a pair of tongs took a live coal from the altar and touched it to his mouth.

"Behold," he said, "this has touched your lips; your guilt is taken away, and your sin forgiven" (Isa. 6:7).

The New Testament has a parallel story in the life of Peter (Luke 5:1–10). When Jesus was being pressed by the crowd at the lake of Gennesaret, he stepped into a fisherman's boat at the shore and asked the fisherman, who happened to be Peter, to row out from the land.

After speaking to the people from the boat, Jesus asked Peter to row out into the deep and let down his nets. Although Peter protested that he had fished all night and caught nothing, he did as the Lord directed. After letting down his nets he caught so many fish that he had to call to his partners for help.

After filling two boats so full that they began to sink, Peter, like Isaiah, was smitten with guilt. When confronted so forcefully by the presence of the divine, Peter fell down at Jesus' knees and said, "Depart from me, for I am a sinful man, O Lord." As with Isaiah, this experience initiated Peter's call to the ministry. "Do not be afraid," Jesus said to him; "henceforth you will be catching men."

But Peter's guilt returned one somber night and, like Isaiah's, centered on his use of the tongue. After Jesus' arrest three years later, Peter was in the courtyard of the high priest's house where Jesus was being held. There he denied three times—out of fear—that he even knew Jesus when he was questioned by the high priest's servants. At that moment Peter caught sight of the Lord looking at him, and Peter left the courtyard and "wept bitterly" (Luke 22:54–62).

His reconciliation took place after Jesus' resurrection when Peter and some other disciples were fishing. Again, after working all night they caught nothing. At daybreak Jesus called to them from the shore to cast their nets again, this time on the right side of the boat, and they were overwhelmed by the amount of fish caught in the nets.

Peter was once more overcome with guilt. It was the same experience he had had the day Jesus called him. Jesus had told him then, Do not be afraid, and now fear had moved him to deny with his tongue that he was Jesus' disciple. Impulsively he put on his clothes and jumped into the water to wade ashore to meet Jesus.

Jesus said nothing to the guilty Peter about his denials. Rather, he invited the disciples to eat breakfast with him on the beach. After they had eaten, Jesus looked at Peter and asked, "Simon, son of John, do you love me?" Peter said, "Yes, Lord." Jesus asked him the same question two more times—once for each denial—and then, as at the beginning, gave him a calling: "Feed my sheep" (John 21:15–17). Peter was forgiven and reaffirmed in his discipleship. His lips, like Isaiah's, were cleansed.

Behind Peter's false use of his tongue was fear. Jesus saw that problem in Peter at the beginning. It is fear that usually keeps us quiet when we should speak and causes us to lie when we can no longer be quiet. Though he failed miserably to live up to his promise to support Jesus in his sufferings, Peter was forgiven. And with that forgiveness came the call to a new life— "Feed my sheep."

Forgiveness for Self

Forgiveness is first of all for oneself. It is received from God through repentance. Isaiah's "I am a man of unclean lips" and Peter's "I am a sinful man" are the confessions of repentance. Both were spoken with deep conviction. They felt the pain of their guilt.

Repentance is different from an apology, which can be glibly given. "OK, I'm sorry," one says, and that's supposed to end it. Just say the right words and the harm is over.

Isaiah and Peter repented of their *sin*. People don't seem to sin anymore. They don't lie, steal, cheat. Instead they admit to poor judgment, errors, mistakes, misunderstandings, or even "getting carried away." All these questionable activities are excusable. Who doesn't make mistakes? Or have bad judgment? Or get carried away by good intentions? Apologies are for the excusable wrongs. We use all kinds of euphemisms to keep these wrongs in the area of the understandable.

Take lying as an example. I heard a radio commentator defend a person who had on his own admission deliberately given false information to Congress. This commentator used the following four words to describe this false witness: dissemble, misinform, misspeak, and mislead. Never once did she say *lie*. One can understand and excuse a person who dissembles much easier than one who lies.

Conflicts clear up faster when we call our behavior by its right name. Or, as we say, call a spade a spade. This is because forgiveness is what is needed in these conflicts since forgiveness is for the inexcusable—the un-understandable. Apologies are sufficient for misspeaking. Repentance is needed for lying. Excusing and understanding are sufficient for getting carried away; forgiveness is needed for cheating. Forgiveness is all that can resolve our guilt over our cruelty, jealousy, desire to hurt, deliberate lying, and other evils.

Repentance begins when we identify both with the pain of the other's hurt and with our own guilt over that pain. First we need to use our tongues in prayer and describe to God, with all the feelings that go with it, our compassion for the one whom we have hurt with our words; then, in the same total-person genuineness, use our tongues to describe the guilt that we feel.

Then comes the time to listen to God. Like Isaiah and Peter, hear God speak the good news of your forgiveness. "Your guilt is taken away; your sin is forgiven." Since God wants to give it, receive it; let forgiveness take over. Since it feels good to be forgiven, use your tongue to express your gratitude.

Now you are ready to reach out to the other and confess your sinful ways to the one who is hurt. Confess to this person as you did to God. You don't have to make any excuses or appeal to any mitigating circumstances. For the forgiveness you desire does not depend on the excusability of the offense.

Then ask for forgiveness. It may take longer than it takes God to give it, but wait for it. The person may need to express anger toward you first. Let it come— for after that will come the reconciliation.

Forgiveness for Others

Forgiveness is also something we give to others. When we do, it is really giving to them what has first been given to us by God. It may be hard to forgive— particularly when we have been deeply hurt or humiliated or rejected—but it is *possible*, because we believe in a God who forgives.

But as the one from whom we ask forgiveness may have to first express anger against us, so also we have to do the same with the one we need to forgive. Now is the time to do it and do it right—using an I message rather than a you message and keeping your responsibility for your feelings while you continue to be honest about expressing them.

Only then may the other realize how much his or her behavior affected you. Only then may the other fully understand the consequences of this behavior in the relationship. Forgiveness comes more easily—and genuinely—after one has put words to the anger and hurt, satisfied that all that needed to be said was said.

Forgiveness that is given out of "Christian duty" often comes at the expense of stuffing our feelings of hurt and anger. Such forgiveness is bestowed through clenched teeth. Since one's own need for expression has not been met, this forced forgiveness conceals a desire for retaliation. When an opportunity comes, retaliation will be swift and impulsive.

Forgiveness is for our sake as well as for the other. Those who withhold forgiveness because they want instead to retaliate against the other—through cutting words, sullen silence, or diminished affection—are increasing negative feelings within themselves that can make them ill. Not only are they robbing themselves of any joy in their relationships, they are also poisoning their own state of mind and body through their resentment. We need to forgive the other for our own sake as well as theirs. As Kierkegaard said, not only the forgiven are blessed but also the forgivers.

Forgiveness—reconciliation—allows newness to enter into *both* lives. As forgiveness breaks our bonds with our destructive pasts, so also it provides a fresh start for the relationship. This means a new use of the tongue. Since forgiveness itself is a miracle, what it produces in the lives of the forgiven and the forgivers is also miraculous. No wonder Paul Tillich said, "Nothing greater can happen to a human being than that he or she is forgiven" (*The New Being*, p. 7; New York: Charles Scribner's Sons, 1955).

Forgiveness makes possible the congruence in the use of the tongue that James in his judgment on the tongue sees as lacking. For those who are reconciled with God, themselves, and each other, there is no need to use their tongues to curse, but plenty of need to use them to bless. The spring can pour forth only the fresh water.

At least some of the time! Perfection is always beyond us. In fact, the more we grow in our potential for change, the more we see into our *imperfections*. This is why there is—and will continue to be—a need on the part of all of us for forgiveness.

12

We Don't Talk About It

When eighteen-year-old Mona came to me for counseling, I asked about her family. Besides her folks she mentioned three siblings, in a family in which she was the youngest. "How much difference is there between you and your siblings?" I asked.

"There's two years between me and my brother and then two more years to my sister and then two more years to my older brother," she replied.

"So your parents had their four children in a six-year span," I said.

Mona hesitated and frowned. "Not exactly," she said.

When I asked her to explain, I realized by her expression that I had moved into a painful area.

"We've never talked about this at home, but my dad had been married before and had a daughter," she said. "I only know this because my older brother told me. Even though she is my half-sister, I never knew her, but my brother remembers her very well. My brother said she ran away when she was about fifteen. When my dad finally found her she was working as a prostitute. I guess she told my dad to get lost. It must have hurt him deeply, but he never talks about it."

"I sense you feel uncomfortable telling me this," I said.

"Yes," she said, "it's like I was saying something that shouldn't be said."

Avoiding the Unpleasant

"We don't talk about it." This is the way too many families deal with painful experiences. It could be a death of a child or a drinking problem of a spouse that no one can face. Or a sexual problem between spouses that they do not talk about. Or a teenage child who is using drugs, or a child who is abused physically or sexually by someone in the family—or the extended family.

Why don't some families talk about these painful realities? Perhaps because family members—particularly the parents—are too hurt to deal with them. A child who is abused may fear that nobody will believe him or her. Or each may be too uneasy about the consequences of talking. Can they handle their feelings—or can the others handle theirs—if they come to the fore?

We are conditioned by family and community mores not to talk about painful realities. The implication of this conditioning is that if these realities are not talked about, they may go away—or if they are talked about, they may get worse.

An Obstacle to Family Intimacy

This reluctance to talk about painful issues in the family is as large an obstacle to family intimacy as put-down language. We even use our tongues to facilitate this avoidance. We know what to say to keep from talking about *it*. We become experts in talking around an issue rather than to it. We grow skillful in speaking generally rather than specifically to evade the sore spots.

We are sensitized to use our tongues to distract attention from the untalked-about subject. Whenever the conversation threatens to approach it, we know how to select substitute issues upon which to focus and are quick to recognize tangents we can take to safer ground.

It was only my assumption based on what she had told me that moved Mona to tell me the whole story of her siblings. So long as it was not obvious that she had not shared with me the whole story, Mona could leave it go. But her need to be accurate was unsatisfied by my verbalized assumption. Her words "not exactly" opened the door to mention the unmentionable.

Families tend to avoid the tension of bringing up a painful issue in favor of not talking about it in the hope that it will become dormant. But of course this doesn't happen, since the subject's intensity as a live issue is the reason it is avoided. So it becomes a symbol of the inability of the family to deal with serious problems. With such limitations placed on their conversation, family relationships tend to grow more superficial rather than intimate.

Talking About Painful Issues

Even as the tongue can be used to distract conversation from painful issues, so also it can be used to address these issues. There is no more direct way to deal with difficult problems than to verbalize them.

Elihu, Job's fourth counselor, did precisely this for Job. In his agony ever his calamities Job had been asking a very difficult question. How, he wanted to know, was he any better off for having lived a life committed to God than if he had not? If such calamities could happen to one who had been faithful to God, what was the advantage in being faithful?

It is an old question and a new question. Why do bad things happen to good people? Rabbi Harold Kushner took Job's ancient question and dealt with it in his book *When Bad Things Happen to Good People*. The response to the book was phenomenal, showing that people in our modern western world are wrestling with the same problem as this ancient easterner.

Job's initial counselors, Eliphaz, Bildad, and Zophar, couldn't "hear" Job's question. It was too disturbing even to consider. Their whole worldview depended on not questioning the justice of the universe. If Job was the victim of many calamities, then his commitment to God must be questioned, and not God's fairness.

For the three friends the universe was affirmed by God's rewarding the righteous and punishing the wicked. Even if it appeared that in some instances the righteous were suffering and the wicked were prospering, this would be short-lived. Justice would prevail.

To all of this Job said in effect, "Baloney!" The evidence is in the opposite direction—the wicked prosper and the righteous suffer. "What is the Almighty that we should serve him?" he asked. "And what profit do we get if we pray to him? . . . One dies in full prosperity, being wholly at ease and secure. . . . Another dies in bitterness of soul, never having tasted of good" (Job 21:15, 23, 25).

But Elihu was different. He faced Job's difficult question. He *said* it. "You ask, 'What advantage have I? How am I better off than if I had sinned?' " (Job 35:3). It takes courage to put a difficult issue or question into words. By restating Job's question as he asked it, Elihu was demonstrating the courage to deal with it. In fact, after stating it, Elihu said, "I will answer you and your friends with you" (35:4). Elihu was critical of these friends because, "they had found no answer, although they had declared Job to be in the wrong" (32:3).

After saying he would deal with Job's difficult question, Elihu proceeded to do so. Troubles come to all people, he said, and not just to the wicked or the righteous. The difference is in how people respond to these troubles. All may cry for help in the multitude of their oppressions, but only those who are committed to God can cry for a specific kind of help. "Where is God my Maker, who gives songs in the night?" (35:10).

"Songs" is the Old Testament symbol for joy and peace; "night" is a symbol for trouble and pain. The believer's advantage over the unbeliever in a day of calamity is that·he or she can pray for songs in the night—and not simply for the removal of the night. The believer, because he or she believes, can pray for strength to endure, for peace in the midst of pain, for joy in the midst of sorrow.

Job was in conflict with God. The three friends did not want to hear about this conflict. They tried to stifle Job by judging him for *having* the conflict. Elihu let this conflict come into the open through the use of words; he faced it and dealt with it.

In like manner our conflicts with our families need to be verbalized, listened to, accepted, and dealt with. While there may be times when it is best to avoid dealing with a family conflict, such as when other pressing issues or needs claim priority, these conflicts sooner or later must come out in verbal openness. They need to find expression even though our personal flaws are exposed in the process. They resolve themselves better in the potential light of speaking than in the darkness of silence.

Most families have unpleasant issues which at least some in the family don't choose to talk about. In-law irritations that are submerged in silence tend to come out in conflicts between the spouses. Conflicts over discipline of the children—who disciplines? when? how?—become absorbed into other problems in the marital relationship when they are not dealt with directly. These problems need to be talked about to be resolved. Otherwise they will simply be *fought* about.

The same is true with personal discipline. When we have difficulty managing ourselves—whether in regard to time, or alcohol, or money, or food, or difficult duties—we are also afflicting others in the family with our indulgences.

The best way to focus on these conflicts is Elihu's way: First, verbalize them to another; next, express your determination to work on the problems; and then brainstorm with the other on ways to do this. This verbalizing may begin with a counselor, but ultimately it needs to take place also with those involved in the conflict.

This kind of verbal openness can lead to genuine acceptance between those involved. In such exchanges one sees the person behind the behavior problems. The result of this deeper sharing is usually an increase in the intimacy of the relationship.

These positive results of dealing with conflicts can happen even when the conflicts are of long standing. Bud was already a father himself when through a workshop in human relationships he realized that he and his own father had much unfinished business. Bud also knew that his father seemed psychologically incapable of taking any initiative to deal with this unfinished business, even though he was probably as aware of it as Bud.

So Bud took the initiative. Knowing his father's love

of fishing he arranged a fishing trip together. The first evening at their campfire Bud used an I message with his father. "I know it's hard for us to talk. But I have a lot of feelings regarding us that I need to talk about. I wonder if you'd be good enough to listen?" The father was obviously apprehensive but gave a minimal assent.

Since they had no way in which to withdraw from each other, Bud and his father finally broke through the old taboos of not talking about their problems. By the end of the three days, a new relationship began to emerge which not only Bud felt good about but also his father. He used an old cliché to express it. "Why do we have to get old before we get smart?"

With Olive it was her brother. From the day he entered the family as a baby they had never gotten along. "He was just born at the wrong time for me," she said candidly. Even as adults they spent as little time together as possible. But Olive had had a renewal experience of her Christian faith and began praying for her brother, and particularly for the improvement of their relationship.

Like Bud she decided to take the initiative. She invited her brother to her house, leaving plenty of time for them to be alone. She told him what she wanted—to feel better about him and their relationship. The brother was at first defensive, letting her see his stored-up anger toward his mean older sister. Olive listened. Her goal was not to defend herself but to form a new relationship.

After a while, having met no resistance to his accusations, the brother began to "hear" Olive. He saw she was genuinely interested in rectifying things. After three hours of increasingly warming conversation, Olive couldn't restrain herself; she threw her arms around her brother. Though startled, her brother responded with his own hug. Soon they were crying tears of joy over what had happened to them.

If you are in a similar situation to Bud or Olive and decide to initiate action to resolve old conflicts with family members that were never talked *about*, even though there was a lot of negative talk *around*, leave room and time for the other's defensiveness. Since you took the initiative, the other is somewhat disadvantaged in the beginning. So allow for time to adjust. Listen. Show understanding. Be open and vulnerable and candid.

Confession rarely comes quickly in these sessions. Only when the other feels safe enough to see his or her role in the conflict can there even begin to be an admission of wrongdoing. But the initiator's open and obvious vulnerability can stimulate the needed insight that the other needs. What is there to defend against in such unoffensive behavior? So the other is inclined at this point to acknowledge some responsibility as well.

Before you begin such an encounter, do as Olive did—pray about it. Pray for yourself, for the other, for the relationship, and for the encounter. Take the trust of your prayer with you into the encounter. It will keep you conscious of another Presence. You will realize that God also wants reconciliation and that God is with you.

Conclusion

Putting words to our feelings with I as the subject begins the process of breaking down the barriers that divide us in the midst of our families—that create loneliness where there should be intimacy. In place of these barriers we will receive an increased sense of belonging—to each other and to the family.

This sense of belonging is vital to family identity. Our home is the setting where we most need to feel safe, secure, and loved unconditionally. Being outwardly safe, inwardly secure, and loved are universal human needs. They are to be provided by the family into which we human beings are born.

It is in this setting—from the biological family to the spiritual family as this is realized in the church as a congregation—that God's love is received unconditionally. The Christian faith is the faith of the incarnation. As God was revealed in Jesus, so God continues to be revealed through those who are reconciled through forgiveness. This revelation begins at our beginning—symbolized by our baptism—in the biological family and in the church family.

In pursuing this goal of reconciliation the tongue fulfills its major purpose, which is to facilitate our knowing each other. Through putting words to our feelings, we deepen the experience of intimacy of mind and spirit within the family. We also enhance the physical intimacies of marriage and family by our use of words to accompany, to label, to enrich these tangible though nonverbal communications.

"So the tongue is a little member and boasts of great things" (James 3:5). In fulfilling its major purpose of revealing ourselves to one another, this boasting is valid. For what is greater, really, than human intimacy?